CONCILIUM

THEOLOGY IN THE AGE OF RENEWAL

CONCILIUM

CONCILIUM/VOL. 37

CHURCH HISTORY

PROPHETS IN THE CHURCH

edited by ROGER AUBERT

VOLUME 37

CONCILIUM
theology in the age of renewal

PAULIST PRESS
NEW YORK, N.Y. / GLEN ROCK, N.J.

Library of Congress Catalogue Card Number 68-57877

Suggested Decimal Classification: 270

Paulist Press assumes responsibility for the accuracy of the English translations in this Volume.

PAULIST PRESS
EXECUTIVE OFFICES: 304 W. 58th Street, New York, N.Y. and 21 Harris-
town Road, Glen Rock, N.J.
Publisher: John A. Carr, C.S.P.
General Manager: Alvin A. Illig, C.S.P.
Asst. General Manager: Thomas E. Comber, C.S.P.

EDITORIAL OFFICES: 304 W. 58th Street, New York, N.Y.
Editor: Kevin A. Lynch, C.S.P.
Managing Editor: Urban P. Intondi

Printed and bound in the United States of America by
Wickersham Printing Co., Lancaster, Pa.

CONTENTS

vii

PART II

DOCUMENTATION CONCILIUM
Office of the Executive Secretary
Nijmegen, Netherlands

PREFACE

Roger Aubert/*Louvain, Belgium*

For most human beings a prophet is a man who foretells the future. But today the term is also used more frequently in a much wider sense and then refers to someone who does not hesitate to query certain elements of the "establishment" in which they have grown up, or even to query the whole system of the establishment and to suggest new forms or ideas better adapted to the arrival of a new age. Thus we talk of Péguy as a prophet or about the prophetic mission of Karl Marx.

Basically, this second meaning is as traditional as the first. In the Old Testament, to be a prophet of God meant not merely to announce future events but also, and even mainly, in the name of God to proclaim God's judgment on the situation of this earth and to show how this situation fits in with God's plan for this world. In this perspective the prophet is, as Congar put it,[1] "the man who does not allow the means to become an end, the outward forms to be pursued and served for their own sake; the man who constantly reminds us that the real truth of the present lies further and at a higher level than the present, and who fiercely points to the spirit that lies behind every shape of letter." The prophet is particularly sensitive to historical changes; he is en-

[1] Y. Congar, *Vraie et fausse réforme dans l'Eglise* (Unam Sanctam 20, Paris, 1950), pp. 196-226.

1

dowed with the gift of interpreting the "signs of the times" before others and for the sake of others. With an acute understanding of new needs and new opportunities, he opposes, sometimes violently, the tendency to treat an established institution or phase, at a given point in history, as if it were definitive. He attacks the false apparent reality in order to rediscover the real reality.

Secular history knows of a number of such prophets. So does religious history, even in the most institutionalized Churches. Modern religious phenomenology likes to contrast, sometimes too systematically, the "type" of the *priest* and that of the *prophet*. The priest represents those members of a Church who consider themselves responsible for the maintenance of doctrine, the ecclesial structure and traditional forms of worship, while the "prophet" represents those who consider themselves to have been charged directly by God with pronouncing God's judgment on the failures of the Church or with encouraging a more or less radical reform in order to adjust the Church to a new historical situation.

We must, of course, not oppose priesthood and prophecy or office and charisma too absolutely, as was sometimes done by Protestant historians at the end of the last century. Even the Old Testament shows that prophets like Jeremiah or Ezekiel were priests, and, much closer to our own time, one would not hesitate to describe as prophets, in the second sense mentioned above, such men as John XXIII, Cardinal Suhard or Patriarch Maximos IV. Nor is it quite correct to say that there is almost inevitably a conflict between prophets and priests: Francis of Assisi and Dominic were supported, in their courageous attempts to bring about an aggiornamento, by Pope Innocent III and several of his cardinals, as Fr. Lebbe found support in Pius XI and some leading figures of the *Congregatio de Propaganda fide* when he pleaded for a radical reassessment of missionary methods. Nevertheless, it is true that the history of the Church shows a permanent tension between the prophetic attempts at renewal and that temptation to yield to formalism and ritualism which so easily besets the priesthood. One can only expect that this tension is more often and more acutely felt in the Roman Catholic Church because of her heavy structuralization and her increasing insistence throughout the centuries on the principle of authority and the practical advantages of centralization. But the existence of tensions is not necessarily an evil but rather a sign of life, of dynamism, of resistance to that sclerosis which threatens all institutions.

Moreover, the place of prophecy within the Church can be theologically justified on genuinely Catholic lines. One of the major themes of contemporary ecclesiology is, in fact, the statement that Christ wanted the whole Church, the whole of the People of God and not only the hierarchy, to be associated with him in the realization of the divine plan for humanity, and Vatican Council II's *Constitution on the Church* was conceived on these lines. After mentioning in n. 12 that "the holy People of God shares also in Christ's prophetic office by spreading a living witness to him, particularly by means of a life of faith and charity", the text says somewhat later on in the same paragraph: "It is not only through the sacraments and Church ministries that the same Holy Spirit sanctifies and leads the People of God and enriches it with virtues. Allotting his gifts 'to everyone according as he will' (1 Cor. 12, 11), he distributes special graces among the faithful of every rank. By these gifts he makes them fit and ready to undertake the various tasks or offices advantageous for the renewal and upbuilding of the Church." Even if one is determined to affirm the institutional character of the Church which received her structures through a positive act of Christ, it remains no less true that it is the Spirit of Christ who constitutes her permanently and who acts with sovereign freedom, where and when he will, even outside the visible boundaries of the Church.

This creative dynamism is born of the spontaneity of both nature and grace, and it raises prophets from age to age in order to disentangle the pure Gospel from the accretions of institutional forms exposed to petrifaction, yet without sacrificing anything that is definitive because established by God himself. This dynamism finds outlets in many different ways, such as the foundation of new religious orders or the creation of new forms of apostolate as well as the introduction of new forms of spirituality which, in spite of being adapted to a changing society, remain within the essential tradition or, in the intellectual field, by attempting fresh interpretations of Christ's eternal message which agree better with the mental structures of a given age or environment. In this sense, the prophet is seen as turned toward the future, not in order to foretell one or other particular event but to guide the development of the People of God toward the fulfillment of God's designs, giving more striking expression to those aspirations for renewal that matured in the community of believers. Bearing witness to the true Church against his time and against certain deformations of the Church of his time, the prophet, supported in his life and activity by a small group of those that understood him and will ensure the continuity of his message, plays an indispensable part in the Church, throughout her history, a part that is as important and permanent as that of the hierarchy. His constant demand for a return to the sources and for reaching beyond the present is, like Bergson's "summons of the hero", the condition *sine qua non* of an "open" religion.

Because he disturbs established security, the prophet will no doubt frequently meet with hostility from within the institution where he fulfills his function, and while he may achieve official recognition late in life or after his death, he usually begins by being the victim of hidden or overt persecution. But this is a law of life which he must have the courage to face. It is, however, important that this prophetic role should be authentic.

Throughout the history of the Church there have been a number of visionaries who were convinced that they had a mission and have been the cause of many a catastrophe. The criterion for this authenticity is, on the one hand, conformity to the Gospel, and, on the other, the desire not to engage in open conflict with that Church which one means to reform in the name of Christ. Even if one thinks of the Church as essentially a charismatic body, the last word cannot be left to uncontrolled individual

enthusiasm. We must avoid the two dangers of a juridical legalism and of a Church of enthusiasts, and steer our course along
the difficult line of "order in charity". The tragedy of some
prophets, whose original impulse was sound and even saintly,
was that they did not have the necessary patience to obey that
law—and one may add, the necessary humility. One may well
ask, of course, whether in many cases they did not lack this
indispensable patience simply because they were blinded by their
awareness of the urgency of the mission to which they felt themselves called, and were brought to the end of their tether by the
resistance, just as often more blind than culpable, of the institutional authorities whose apathy they tried rightly to overcome.

Concrete examples of these observations can be found on
many a page of Church history, and they help us to understand
better the various aspects of Christian prophecy, its dangers and
failures as well as its positive achievements and its indispensable
function. In this volume we could of course not possibly deal
with them all, or even with the main ones. Without even mentioning the numerous reforms that will be left out, a number of
attempts that could be described as prophetic in one way or
another have been omitted for shortage of space, although a
reform (such as the Gregorian) often appears as a return to the
past while the prophet looks to the future in order to discover
there new features that might help the Church to fulfill her mission in new conditions.

With regard to other "prophetic attempts" mentioned above,
we have, for instance, certain reactions of the old monachism
against an establishment whose advantages concealed its dangers
for many, or the confused but inspired and genuinely construc-
tive attempt of Joachim of Fiore to rediscover the true sense of
monachism. It was judged unnecessary to recall once again the
tragic but well-known cases of a Luther or a Calvin during the
religious crisis of the beginning of the 16th century, or the case
of Lamennais who, even before 1830, foresaw most of the problems that confront 20th-century Christians. The few cases dealt
with, taken from various periods in history and not limited to the

Catholic Church, will help at least to start a reflection, not based on abstract terms, but on concrete examples. These examples would have been still more significant if space had allowed us to place them in their environment of the world and the Church of their age, because we are not dealing with isolated and disembodied figures—the treatment often given them in traditional hagiography—but with men molded in a quite definite cultural and religious milieu, men who, at a given moment, reacted against this milieu in order to transform it because they were urged on by the Spirit. One *Concilium* volume cannot be a substitute for a definitive volume of Church history. Theologians today are occasionally inclined to forget that Church history is one of the *loci theologici* (sources of theology) from where they should start to work out their theories. If we have at least made them aware of this fact, we shall have achieved our aim.

Part I
Articles

Giulio Basetti-Sani, O.F.M./St. Bonaventure, N.Y.

Francis of Assisi

hristian tradition recognizes St.
Francis of Assisi as the man sent
by God to bring about a renewal
of the spirit of the Gospel in the Church. Francis' prophetic
mission was intended to help Christendom to overcome the twofold crisis which occurred at the end of the 12th and the beginning of the 13th centuries, namely, the problem of the relations
between the Church and the Empire, and the presence of Islam.
The solutions adopted at the time seemed justified from the
human point of view, but they were not based on the supernatural principles of the Gospel. The "Voice of God" spoke in the
form of the words and actions of St. Francis—a man who never
became more than a deacon. Few of his contemporaries fully
understood the prophetic import of his message. After a lapse of
more than 700 years we are in a better position today to appreci-
ate St. Francis; in fact, the solutions put forward by the Church
in Vatican Council II for the two problems which provoked such
a crisis for medieval Christendom provide a parallel to the solution suggested by Francis of Assisi.[1]

[1] Cf. Y. Congar, "Poverty in Christian Life amidst an Affluent Society,"
in Concilium 15(1966), pp. 49-70; R. Caspar, "La religion Musulmane,"
in Les relations de l'Eglise avec les religions non-chrétiennes (Unam
Sanctam 61, Paris 1966), pp. 201-36; G. Basetti-Sani, "Per un dialogo tra
cristiani e musulmani: Il Concilio Vaticano II e la religione dell'Islam,"
in La Scuola Catt. (1966), pp. 267-89; idem, "The New Spirit toward

Crisis in the Church

The life of Christians at the end of the 12th and the beginning of the 13th centuries must be seen against the background of the social and cultural progress being made in Europe. "The Church is in constant need of being corrected and reformed",[2] and as a result of the Third Lateran Council the newly formed lower classes saw a reawakening of the Gospel spirit and a desire for complete commitment to the Gospel. Various movements arose as evidence of this revival: the Waldensians, the Pauperes of Lyons and various other new sects. But within the Church it was the Franciscan and Dominican movements which represented the authoritative response to this desire for renewal.

The Holy Roman Empire and the Church

Gregory VII hoped that he had achieved lasting harmony and cooperation between the papacy and the Empire. But events at the end of the 12th century were to prove that ideas still differed on the relationship between the Empire and the Church. The Church saw the unity of Western Christendom as centered on the Holy See in Rome; the pope was the summit and source of all human power, and the Christian kingdoms within the Holy

---

Islam," in *World Mission* 17(1966), pp. 27-52; for the biographers of St. Francis, Thomas of Celano, Giuliano da Spira and St. Bonaventure cf. the original Latin text edited in *Analecta Franciscana* X (1940).

[2] *Alexander III* (*Mansi,* Collect. concil., XXII), p. 212 cf. P. Zerbi, *Papato, Impero e "Respublica Christiana"* (Milan, 1955); A. Fliche, *La chrétienté Romaine,* in Fliche-Martin, *Histoire de l'Englise* (Paris, 1935ff.); M. Maccarone, *Chiesa et Stato nella dottrina di Papa Innocenzo III* (1960). Maccarone considers Innocent III as the high point of papal power. Other historians, such as Dietrich Kemp and Hélène Tillmann, see it rather as being under Innocent IV. Personally, I find the position of Maccarone more convincing. There was absolutely no one in the time of Innocent III who dared to defy the authority of the papacy, not even the Emperor Frederick, who did however challenge the authority of Innocent IV. Innocent no longer felt himself to be secure in Rome, which was after all his own city, and was obliged to set out for Genoa and then Lyons. The series of disputes which followed the death of the emperor show that the papal authority in the temporal order was no longer accepted without discussion as it had been in the days of Innocent III.

Roman Empire ought to acknowledge their dependence on the supreme pontiff, and this not only in the spiritual order but also in the temporal. The imperial attitude was rather that Christendom had as its center and leader the German Empire, and the Church and papacy were powers subordinate to the supreme imperial authority. These two opposing approaches were often a source of conflict and had serious consequences in the pastoral sphere.

Furthermore, the political scene had altered considerably since the time of Gregory VII. The Church, of course, had taken cognizance of this development and had established relations with the individual nations which were independent of the Empire. In these contacts the papacy did not keep merely to purely spiritual affairs but frequently concerned itself also with temporal masters. Aware of the strength of the unity of the baptized peoples on occasions when the civil arm was powerless, the popes, like supreme feudal lords, sometimes initiated enterprises whose aim was to defend Christendom, to the detriment, however, of the Church's spiritual and apostolic mission. For the Church, like Jesus himself, is continually subject to the temptations of Satan ("I will give you all this power and the glory of these kingdoms . . ." : Lk. 4, 6), with the aim of making the Church forget the kingdom of God. The Third Lateran Council had appealed to the clergy to abstain from any political activity. Higher authority in the Church did not always in fact set a good example; ambition, a desire for power and, above all, a desire for wealth were much in evidence.

Historians usually consider the pontificate of Innocent III as the apogee of the papacy; the Church appears to be at the high point of her power and influence, as she dominates the Empire, the kings of Christendom and the Emperor with her considerable magnificence and wealth. But this situation, which today is called "triumphalism", does not mean that the Gospel spirit was therefore flourishing in the Church. The tension that existed between the temporal power of the Empire and the kingdoms of Christendom as opposed to the activity of the Church, which was not always confined to the spiritual order, constituted a serious danger for the Church. To resolve this tension, God sent Francis, with his call to the absolute poverty demanded by the Gospel, in an attempt to free the Church from the temptation to pursue temporal power.

The Call to Perfect Poverty

St. Bonaventure wrote: "Francis is a new manifestation of the saving grace of Christ to recall men to a complete imitation of Christ, and to lead them to desire and pursue the things of God." [3] In the words of Christ ("Go, Francis, and repair my house which is falling into ruin") God gave Francis his prophetic mission to restore the spirit of the Gospel. It was the Church of Christ which was in need of repair, and Innocent III recognized in Francis the mendicant brother whom he had seen in a dream holding up the Lateran Basilica. [4]

To oppose the continual attraction of temporal power and aggrandizement, Francis preached absolute and complete evangelical poverty. The saint did not descend into the marketplace to denounce in the name of the Gospel the greed and pride of certain churchmen, as was the practice of some so-called reformers. Rather, he used his own kind example and gentle persuasion to recall the whole Church, head and members, to the heights of evangelical spirituality so that she might be purely and simply herself, concerned only with the things of God.

This message of Francis, contained in his preaching and example, was put into writing by one of his first disciples, as the heritage which he left not only to his own brethren, but to the whole Church. The famous opusculum *Sacrum Commercium B. Francisci cum Domina Paupertate* contains this message which has been faithfully passed on to us by Fra Giovanni Parenti, General of the Order. There have been many interpretations of

---

[3] St. Bonaventure, *Legenda Major* (Prol. n. 1, p. 557). In spite of everything, there survived various groups of laymen and clergy who genuinely desired and sought after a truly apostolic life.

[4] *Idem*, c. 2. n. 1, p. 563; Thomas of Celano, *Vita secunda*, n. 17, p. 141.

the *Sacrum Commercium:* a poetic allegory encouraging the Franciscans to a life of poverty; a blueprint for the rigid following of St. Francis; an idealistic program for life in the world; a strange idyll, the dream of a very saintly monk; an innocent romantic poem, like a wedding song, written to draw the brethren to a love of poverty.

Perhaps it was Paul Sabatier more than anyone else who appreciated that it was intended for the whole Church rather than for Francis' brethren alone, since it contains the same ideas as St. Bernard; it attacks the wealth of the Church and the desire for greater riches, and maintains that the apostolic power of the pope and bishops was given to them not that they may lord over others, but for the sanctification of men.[5] The Lady Poverty of the *Sacrum Commercium* is not, as is often thought, an allegorical figure of the virtue of poverty, but rather the Church herself, *Sponsa Christi.* St. Francis in the presence of Innocent III told the parable of the rich king; he married a beautiful lady, who was however very poor. This lady is the Church, who gives birth to the sons and heirs of Christ.[6] The two "guardians" are the two apostles, Peter and Paul, who reply to St. Francis with passages from their epistles. The city set on the mountain is Jerusalem, the abode of the Church.

Interpreted in this way the *Sacrum Commercium* has all the appearance of St. Francis' testament to the universal Church. His remedy for the crisis in relations between the Church and the Empire was a return to the perfect poverty of the Gospel in order to rebuild the Church, now cleansed and free from any implication of wordly ambition. At the time, this message was not fully understood.[7] It has taken seven centuries, from Innocent III to Paul VI, for the Church to understand that the exercise of the Gospel authority by the vicar of Christ and the successors of the apostles, the bishops, gave them no right to worldly power and

[5] *Sacrum Commercium S. Francisci cum Domina Paupertate* (1929); S. Bernardi, *De consideratione ad Eugenium* (*P.L.* CLXXXII, pp. 757ff., 915ff.).

[6] Celano, *Vita prima*, n. 36, p. 22; *Vita secunda*, n. 16, p. 212.

[7] Cf. Paul VI, *Discorso all' O.N.U.* (Oct. 4, 1965).

no justification for it. If the contemporaries of Francis had understood this, the history of the Church may well have been quite
different, with a more spiritual solution to the serious clashes
there have been between the Church and temporal powers from
the 13th century until today.

Islam and Medieval Christendom

The expansion of the Muslim Empire was the reply of the
Semitic Orient to the Greco-Roman conquest, which had begun
with Alexander the Great. The Christian of the Middle Ages felt
himself to be surrounded by the Muslim world, and he considered Islam as a diabolical force, a political and military threat to
the faith, in the face of which only military strength could guarantee peace and restore the Holy Land to Christian hands. St.
Bernard praised this holy war against the enemies of the cross of
Christ, and he said explicitly that the "soldiers of Christ", the
crusaders, did not commit a crime by killing a Muslim; they were
not *homicidae* but *malicidae*,[8] freeing this world from evil men,
and so giving glory to God. If a soldier dies fighting for Christ,
he is assured of heavenly glory.

The religious character of the Crusades was not so clear to the
Muslims. Rather, they viewed them as the aggression of the
Christian foreigners, the Franks, against Islamic territory, with
the intention of destroying the religion of the prophet. Contrary
to Christian expectations, the Crusades did not weaken Islam;
rather, they gave added strength by enabling the divided parties
to settle their differences. The upshot was greater political unity,
the triumph of Sunnamite orthodoxy over the Fatimite schism,
and a renewal of Arab culture in Syria and Egypt, Damascus and
Cairo regaining their position as the most flourishing centers of
the Muslim world. When Saladin reconquered Jerusalem in
1187, there swept through Islam a renewed feeling of devotion

[8] Cf. S. Bernardi, *Tractatus de Nova Militia* (*P.L.* CLXXXII, pp.
921-931). From the point of view of the psychology and sociology of religion, the Crusades were the exact equivalent of the "Holy War" of Islam,
according to J. Leclerc, *Histoire de la tolérance au siècle de la Réforme*
I (Paris, 1954), p. 104.

and attachment to Jerusalem, since for them, too, it was a holy place, and they now returned to pray on the spot where once had stood the temple of Solomon. Thus Saladin reestablished the rule of "the true believers" over the Holy Land. Hardly had he entered Jerusalem on October 2nd, 1187, the day when Muslims liturgically celebrate the night of Mohammed's ascension, than Saladin gave the order to restore the Mosque of the Rock and the Mosque of al-Aqsa, announcing to the Muslim world that "al-Quds", the Holy City, had now been purified of the presence of the infidel.

In Western Christendom the news of the defeat at Tiberias and the capture of Jerusalem by Saladin was seen by Gregory VIII as the punishment of God in his wrath against his sinful people. Only a renewal in moral life and exceptional penance could obtain the mercy of God and victory over the enemies of the cross of Christ.[9] The call to a new Crusade, repeated by Gregory's successors Clement III and Celestine III, met with an unsatisfactory response.

The new, young Pope Innocent III immediately announced his program of reform for the Church to bring about the liberation of the Holy Land. These two objectives were for him inseparable. In his attitude to Islam he clearly distinguished his political activity, dealing with the Muslim kings and princes through diplomatic channels and recognizing them as sovereigns responsible for the government of their countries, but in his approach to Islam as a religion he viewed it as no less than the work of the devil and the great enemy of the Christian faith. And so the pope commissioned a Florentine, Aimaro de' Corbizzi, Patriarch of the Latins in Jerusalem, to take to the Sultan of Egypt in Cairo, Al-'Adil Saîf el-Dîn, a letter which laid down the pope's moral obligation to free the Holy Land, claiming that in the name of justice the sultan ought to restore that which did not belong to him and had been unlawfully seized by the Muslims; in the event of a refusal, Christendom would be obliged to resort to military measures to liberate the Holy Land.

[9] Epist. *Audite Tremendi* (*Mansi, loc. cit.,* pp. 527-31).

Innocent was to repeat this threat in another letter to the Sultan of Egypt in 1213.[10] But even the pope was persuaded that it was necessary first to destroy by force the political power of Islam which was based on military strength, just as his contemporaries believed that the Crusades were to destroy Islam and realize the prophecy of the Apocalypse (the number 666 was interpreted as being the allotted span of the Muslim religion).

The disaster of the Fourth Crusade (1204) did not shake the conviction that only force of arms would bring about the defeat of Islam; in the mind of the pope the task of reforming the Church was inextricably linked with the liberation of the sepulchre of Christ, so that he was unable to dissociate the military—and distinctly ungospel-like—character of the Crusade from the moral and spiritual renewal of the Church. In his appeal for a new Crusade he said in April, 1213: "The day of the liberation now seems to be at hand. The power of Islam, whose days are indicated in the Apocalypse by the number of the beast, 666 (Apoc. 13, 18), is coming to an end." [11]

Innocent III also maintained the traditional aggressive language, describing the Muslims as *inimici Crucis Christi, perfidi, pessimi,* etc. Even the pope failed to detect the ambiguity in the view, by now two centuries old, that the presence of Islam in Jerusalem was the gravest insult to Jesus Christ, who was thus expelled from the kingdom which he had won with his own blood. If Christians do not defend the cause by reconquering the very home of Christ now in the hands of his enemies, how can they call themselves Christians? The liberation of the Holy Sepulchre was seen as the reward which God was keeping for Christendom when it had undergone a spiritual renewal. Adopting the image of St. Bernard of the "soldier of Christ"—*miles Christi*—the pope exalted the Crusade as a sacred enterprise, closely linked to the passion and death of Christ.[12]

[10] *Acta Innoc. PP. III,* n. 204, p. 44.
[11] Innocentii, *De negotio Terrae Sanctae,* Epist. 28 (*P.L.* CCXVI, p. 818).
[12] "Quia major nunc," in *Mansi, loc. cit.,* pp. 956-60.

But the hopes of the pope and Christendom for the end of Islam were not realized; the prophecies turned out to be untrue and the Muslim religion was not destroyed by the sword of the Christians. Nor for that matter did the Crusades reconcile the "true believers" to the Gospel. The centuries-old association of the violence of the crusades and the *miles Christi* of St. Paul with the passion and death of Christ constituted a grave deviation from the authentic spirit of the Gospel. It was precisely in his passion and death that Christ intended to renounce any violent resistance, and he left the Church an example and model. He did not permit Peter to use his sword, when he could rightly have called to his defense legions of angels. By his words and example, St. Francis was to recall all this to the conscience of medieval Christianity.

The Crusaders and the Gospel

Francis' prophetic mission to Islam can already be glimpsed in the use Thomas of Celano and St. Bonaventure made of the Pauline phrase *miles Christi*. St. Paul wrote in his letter to Timothy: "Put up with your share of difficulties, like a good soldier of Christ Jesus" (2 Tim. 2, 3). Certainly St. Paul did not picture the "soldier of Christ" with sword in hand, intent on the slaughter of the enemies of Christ. As opposed to the soldier of the Roman army or any other, the "soldier of Christ" must not inflict suffering on others by brute force, but is himself called to suffer in union with the passion and death of Christ. To apply the words of St. Paul to a context of war and aggression, as became the custom after St. Bernard even in papal documents, is to betray the true spirit of St. Paul. But when applied to St. Francis, as it was by his first biographers, *miles Christi* takes on its own particular meaning. Any prophet comes with a message and uses the categories of his time to reverse the values contained in those categories. Thus St. Francis, the authentic *miles Christi,* was to lead the Church back to the true meaning of St. Paul's words; his prophetic vocation was in opposition to the ideal of the Crusades, in which the soldiers carried arms marked with the cross of Christ. The vision, in which he saw the palace and arms "bearing the cross of Christ", was the first call he received to his mission of peace and opposition to all violent action taken in the name of Christ.[13]

St. Francis helped Christendom to distinguish religious reform from the warlike Crusades, which were rather intended to conquer Islam by violent means. He announced the peace of the Gospel, which is given from on high, and the victory of Christ, which was achieved by his passion and death. Francis was to show that the Gospel never needs force to defend the rights of God. Islam had implanted in the conscience of medieval Christendom the idea that only by opposing violence with violence and by countering the evil of war with the same means would it be possible to save the faith and render due honor to the cross of Christ. The name of God was used to justify the accumulation of injustice and physical and moral evil which followed in the train of the war. The authority of the papacy had for years presented the Crusades as the means of defense against the enemies of the cross of Christ. St. Francis, as a prophet, appealed instead to the words of Christ: "You will find peace in me. In the world you will have trouble, but be brave; I have conquered the world" (Jn. 16, 33). To the Christians who were intimidated by the presence of the Muslims and imagined that they could conquer Islam by force of arms, St. Francis repeated the message of Christ, and in the name of the Gospel condemned the principle *Vim vi repellere licet,* which has been overthrown by the divine wisdom in the paradox, "Love your enemies; do good to those who hate you" (Lk. 6, 27).

St. Francis was careful to make plain his meaning: the Muslims appear to be our enemies, but the Gospel obliges us to love them. He was fully aware of the force of this divine wisdom, and of the place in the economy of salvation of suffering and death. It was for Francis to announce to all men love and forgiveness for

---

[13] Cf. Celano, *Vita prima,* nn. 5-7, 9-10; St. Bonaventure, *Legenda major,* c. 1, nn. 3-4, p. 619; c. 13, nn. 9-10, p. 620.

the Muslims. This represents a complete reversal of the ordinary policy hitherto adopted by the Church in defending herself against Muslim power. Conscious of the value of the words of Christ, Francis could not consider the Muslims as the "enemies of Christ". For him they are brothers to be brought to the full knowledge of the mystery of Christ by words and deeds which reveal the spirit of the Gospel, and above all by heroic charity, even to the extent of giving himself in the supreme sacrifice of martyrdom. This is the essential core of Francis' prophetic message to Christendom.

His long meditation on the passion and death of Christ had taught him that the salvation of man was the fruit of self-sacrifice and suffering. We must be alive to the equivocation in the biographies of Francis, which represent his journey to Egypt as a participation in the Crusade for the purpose of giving it a "spiritual" content—as if violence could be spiritualized! It is after all essentially a negation of the spirit of the Gospel. In fact, God had sent Francis precisely to bring the Crusades to an end. It is only through love, suffering and humility that the Gospel will conquer the world, Islam included. This is still the message of Francis to Christians today.

St. Francis' Visit to Egypt

As early as 1211 St. Francis wanted to go to Syria, a Muslim country, to bear witness to Christ. But providence disposed otherwise and he could not reach Syria, just as later he did not reach Morocco. Before going to preach to the Muslims, he had first to call Christians to a change of heart. The Fourth Lateran Council was still able to call Christendom to war in the Crusade of which Innocent III himself was to take command and travel to the Orient. But he died at Perugia on July 16, 1216; God did not allow the spectacle of the pope at the head of an army. St. Francis was in Perugia for the funeral of the pope. Very probably he had tried in the name of the Gospel to dissuade the pope from the Crusade. Introduced by Cardinal Ugolino into the presence of Honorius III and the cardinals, Francis spoke on the subject of the Church.[14] His purpose was to explain further his advice to suspend the Crusade and transfer the "Crusade indulgence for the liberation of Jerusalem" to Assisi, the "New Orient", in the shape of the Porziuncula indulgence.

However, by now all was ready for the doomed expedition. Later, the saint asked the pope for permission to go to the camp of the crusaders in Egypt, in an attempt to persuade the leaders —Cardinal Alvaro Pelagio, the papal legate, and King John of Rienne—to accept the peace terms of the sultan, Melek el-Kamel, who was prepared to return Jerusalem, provided that the Christian army retired from Egypt. By this time, in the minds of the Christian leaders the purpose of the Crusade was not the liberation of the Holy City and Palestine, but rather the destruction of Muslim power. St. Francis' presence in the camp of the crusaders was a living condemnation of their violent, warlike spirit. He demanded of the Christians that they should replace violence with meekness, and that instead of hatred and disdain for the Muslims, whom they considered as inferiors and enemies, they should have rather respect and love. In the name of Christ, they should be recognized as brothers and friends; in fact, every Christian should be ready, like St. Francis, to suffer martyrdom for the salvation of the Muslims, whose souls, redeemed by the blood of Christ, were far more precious than the stones of the Holy Sepulchre.

"When he knew with certainty," wrote Thomas of Celano, "that the crusaders were determined to fight, deep sorrow came over St. Francis. And he said to his companion [Brother Illuminato of Rieti]: 'If they do indeed begin the battle, God has made it known to me that it will result in a defeat for the Christains. Now if I say this, they will consider me mad. On the other hand, if I keep silent, I shall not be able to avoid the condemnaton of my conscience. What do you think I must do?' His companion replied: 'Father, do not be concerned over the judgment of men. You know that it is not the first or last time that you will

[14] Cf. Celano, *ibid.*, nn. 73, 54-55; St. Bonaventure, *Legenda minor*, c. 12, n. 7, p. 613.

be considered mad. Unburden your conscience, and fear God more than man.' The saint went forth, and he solemnly warned the Christians, forbidding them in the name of God to give battle; should they do so, he foretold their defeat. Francis' words, destined to prove only too true, were ridiculed; the men hardened their hearts and did not wish to accept the warning contained in the words of God." [15]

Before Damietta, Francis wept over the useless slaughter caused by the warlike papal legate, who did not recognize in the words of the saint the revelation of the will of God. Unable to grasp the spirit of what Francis had said, the legate had prevented him from going to the sultan to offer peace. Now, after the defeat of August 31, 1219, he allowed St. Francis to go to the Muslim camp. Francis had no other idea than to offer his life as a martyr of Christ in order to obtain grace and enlightenment for his Muslim brethren, in the hope of bringing about the pacification of the Christian and Muslim worlds. But, as Thomas of Celano and St. Bonaventure witness, God was keeping the martyrdom Francis so eagerly sought in Egypt for some years later, on Monte Verna, and this in a form hitherto unheard of: the stigmata.

St. Francis' Dialogue with Islam

When he reached the presence of the sultan, St. Francis asked for a hearing, and invited Islam, in the persons of its learned men, to accept the ordeal by fire, to prove the truth of the Christian faith. The sincerity and gentleness with which the saint and Brother Illuminato of Rieti presented themselves as sent on a mission from God made an immediate and deep impression and won the respect of their hearers. This attitude of humility and genuine Christian goodness had nothing in common with the violent spirit of the crusaders. The religious conscience of Melek el-Kamel, a just and holy man, was ready to accept the witness of a "bearer of the Word of God". Thomas of Celano and Bonaven-

[15] Celano, *Vita secunda*, n. 30, p. 149; G. Basetti-Sani, *Mohammed et Saint Francois* (Ottawa, 1959), pp. 157-65.

ture relate that the sultan immediately recognized the fervor and holiness of the brother, who said nothing in contempt of the person of Mohammed or the Koran. It is very difficult to imagine a medieval Latin Christian in conversation with a Muslim and not showing contempt for his religion and blaspheming his prophet. St. Francis had considerable respect for others, in the true spirit of the Gospel, seeing the finger of God everywhere, even among the Muslims. He declared himself ready to accept the invitation of the sultan and remain there for the love of Christ, but he expressed his desire to bear witness to his Christian faith by undergoing the ordeal by fire.

The Ordeal at Medina and at Damietta

This gesture of his, in inviting the Muslim doctors to pass through fire with him, if it is to be understood properly as authentic Christian witness, must be related to another similar event (this according to the interpretation of L. Massignon), namely, the meeting at Medina of Mohammed and a delegation of Christians of Nidjrân. They had come under the leadership of their bishop to render homage and submit to the civil authority of Mohammed. After a discussion on the passion of Christ, they were asked to prove the truth of the incarnation and divinity of Christ by the ordeal by fire, *Mubahâla*. Mohammed asked them to pray for the return of Christ as judge and to recognize his mission as prophet. They refused the challenge, saying however that they were ready to negotiate with him. Is it possible that this refusal blocked the way for Mohammed to a full understanding of the mystery of Christ?

This ordeal demanded by Mohammed of the Christians at Medina was now being asked by Francis of the Muslims at Damietta in their turn, as if to make up for the previous faint-hearted refusal. When thus seen in relation with the events at Medina, the gesture of Francis appears as a prophetic announcement of the new attitude which God now required of Christians with regard to Islam: reparation through suffering, witness to the faith through suffering and death, and Christian charity which judges no man but recognizes in all men the gifts of God and loves the Muslims as brethren even to the point of martyrdom. The image of God and the mark of Christ are to be seen in them too, and intercession is to be made for them, pleading for the salvation of their souls.

Francis' suggestion at Damietta was not accepted. The conduct of the sultan and the Muslim doctors, who by their nonacceptance had opened a breach, must be judged in the light of Muslim religious psychology. The events at Medina of the *Mubahâla* and the revelation to be found in the Koran (3, 42-55) persuaded the Muslims that the judgment of God ought not to be anticipated, since on the last day he will reveal the true nature of Christ. Therefore, the refusal of the sultan to accept the test set by Francis does not mean that he despised either the saint or the Christian religion; rather, in accordance with the Muslim religion, he acknowledged the divine origin of Christianity: "I believe that your faith is good and true!" [16]

Norms for Dialogue

To all appearances, the Muslims refused the gift of love offered by St. Francis when he risked his life in the hope of being martyred. In fact, this action of Francis was an illustration of the interior dispositions and the conditions necessary for successful dialogue—namely, love for the Muslim brethren and preparation for the hour of grace by suffering and prayer. His return to Italy was not due to his disillusionment with the Muslims, as St. Bonaventure and Dante would have us believe; rather, precisely because he was convinced that something had to be done, he laid down in the Rule for his followers a two-stage program "for the brothers who wish to go among the Saracens".[17]

The *first stage* consisted of witness and presentation of the

[16] St. Bonaventure, "De. S. Francisco Sermo II," in *Opera Omnia* 9, p. 579; L. Massignon, "La Mubahâla de Médine. Etude sur la proposition d'ordalie faite par le prophète Muhammed aux Chrétiens Balhârith du Najrân, in *Opera Minora* I(Beirut, 1963), pp. 550-572; G. Basetti-Sani, *op. cit.*, pp. 129-54, 163-83.

[17] S. Francisci, *Opuscula* (Regula I, c. 16), pp. 43-46.

Gospel to the Muslims by means of the practice of the Christian virtues: "Let them not be argumentative or contentious, but let them be subject to every creature for the love of God." Their humility, poverty and the gentleness and meekness of their conduct were first to reveal the Gospel as a preparation of the ground for preaching the humiliation and sacrifice of the Son of God. The *second stage* comprised the Good News, the explicit preaching of Christian truth: "When the time comes, they will preach the Father, the Son and the Holy Spirit, and they will be baptized."

Monte Verna: The Martyrdom of Francis

God had accepted Francis' offer of himself and his desire to be martyred on behalf of the Muslims. On Monte Verna he gave him a new, as yet unknown, form of martyrdom, by which for two years he was, as it were, crucified alive as his way of participating in the passion and death of Christ.

Thomas of Celano, St. Bonaventure and the first biographers have left a description of the splendid apparition of Christ in the figure of a winged seraph on Monte Verna in September, 1224. But there has been little emphasis on the connection between the apparition on Verna and the words of Francis at Damietta. The Franciscan tradition has meditated on the mystery of Francis' stigmata for more than 700 years, but it has so far concentrated on its significance for the person of St. Francis, as a supreme form of likeness to Christ, and has thus missed the full meaning of this mysterious apparition, which made such a deep impression on Francis himself. For the first time in history, Christ appeared in the form of a crucified angel—the only "apparition of the crucified Christ in glory". Why did this happen, not in Francis' private cell, but in the setting of a mountain which is reminiscent rather of Sinai and Tabor? And why too did Christ, the crucified, transform Francis likewise into a crucified figure, thus conferring on him the martyrdom he so wanted to suffer for the salvation of the Muslims? Christ's purpose was to make visible in the body of Francis his crucifixion, and so authenticate his prophetic mission within the Church to Islam. This stigmata was to be a witness of the reality of the crucifixion on Calvary to the Muslims, who commonly denied it, following as they did a false interpretation of a Koranic text.

Prof. L. Massignon is very enlightening on this point also. Francis had shown great love for his Muslim brethren by his offering of himself and his acceptance of suffering and by his invitation to Christendom to change its approach to Islam. Now Francis obtained from God a totally unexpected reply to the prayer Mohammed had made on the night of his ascension. Not realizing the true meaning or function of the incarnation, he had prayed that God would reveal himself in the form of an angel. But only Christ can fully reveal the Father (cf. Jn. 3, 31-36). The apparition on Verna, when Christ appeared to Francis as a crucified seraph to make him the living, visible sign of the reality of the crucifixion on Calvary, was in fact the reply to the prayer of Mohammed. Through the wounds of the stigmata of St. Francis, Islam was in a position to be introduced into the mysterious reality of Christ's crucifixion.[18] Verna thus had the effect of relating the dialogue begun at Damietta between Christianity and Islam to the mystery of suffering and the cross, and made of St. Francis the great mediator with God for the salvation of the Muslims.

If the contemporaries of St. Francis did not succeed in understanding the full implications of his prophetic mission, today, in the climate of renewal initiated by Vatican Council II, we are better prepared to accept the full message of St. Francis as he points once again to the poverty taught by the Gospel and calls for greater love and understanding in our approach to the Muslim world.

[18] L. Massignon, in *Les trois prières d'Abraham* (Tours 1935), pp. 17-18, 64.

William Peters, S.J./*Nijmegen, Netherlands*

St. Ignatius Loyola as Prophet

To be quite frank, it seems far-fetched to associate Ignatius of Loyola with the gift of prophecy. One wonders whether the title of this article should be taken seriously. There is little, if any, open protest in his life and in his work. The daring resistance of the prophet against intolerable situations and utterly objectionable practices within the Church is hardly discernible. He is no rebel, no iconoclast. He is not like the prophets of old, sitting at city or temple gate, lamenting that things have come to a shocking pass and loudly clamoring that unless things change, and change quickly, God's wrath cannot be turned away. If prophecy stands for a breakthrough of antiquated formalities, outworn devotions and a fixed pattern of religious behavior, often tainted by false doctrine, idolatry and magic, Ignatius hardly fits the part of a prophet.

In fact, a good case might be made out that he made matters worse. Not only did he not condemn what nowadays is understood by *religio,* but he contributed his own set of rules, regulations and restrictions. No one links the ten parts of the Constitutions which he drew up for the Order he founded with a prophetic vocation, and the book of the Spiritual Exercises (Sp. Ex.) with its detailed methods of how to pray, its rules for doing penance or behaving at table, its examination of conscience twice daily, and so forth, does anything but conjure up the image of a prophet.[1] And if prophecy carries with it a breath of the Spirit blowing where it will (Jn. 3, 8), Ignatius' seemingly relentless insistence on rather indiscriminate self-conquest (Ex. Sp. 21) and killing of the old man expressed by the notorious *agere contra* (acting against: *ibid.*, 97) is enough to do away with any Spirit. In the life of the Church Ignatius cannot be said to stand for the voice of prophecy; he stands for obedience and docility, as his rules for thinking with the Church, the closing words of the Spiritual Exercises (352-370), only serve to underline.

In any survey of Ignatius' life, traces of the true prophet seem very hard to detect. If one holds that he was a great soldier changing his allegiance from an earthly king to Christ the king and as a redoubtable strategist sending his well-trained men right and left to conquer the world for Christ and thus expand the power and the influence of the Church, there cannot be any question of prophecy at all. Even if one does away with this—in our opinion—untenable view and, following the lead of modern scholars,[2] one is prepared to consider him a true mystic and first class organizer—a somewhat startling combination—it remains difficult to discover the prophet. Surely, no one will look upon Ignatius' conversion as a call that can be compared to that of a Moses, Isaiah or Amos, and no one will see in the small band of Parisian students a budding school of prophets. With the excep-

---

[1] The scholarly edition of the Constitutions is published in *Monumenta Historica Societatis Jesu* (MHSJ): *Monumenta Ignatiana, Series tertia*, I-III (Rome, 1934-1938). In quotations and references the Roman numeral, c followed by an Arabic numeral, n also followed by an Arabic numeral and a capital letter indicate respectively the part, chapter, paragraph and declaration. The text of the Spiritual Exercises is found in MHSJ: *Monumenta Ignatiana, Series secunda: Exercitia Spiritualia Sancti Ignatii de Loyola et eorum Directoria*, Matriti 1919; Nova editio, II: Directoria (1540-1594) (Rome, 1955). In referring to the text we shall make use of the numbering found in the Marietti edition of 1928, which has been accepted by modern translators such as Puhl, Corbishley, Courel, Haas, Tesser and others.

[2] The names of Codina, Tacchi Venturi, Astráin, Leturia, Hugo Rahner and Iparraguirre suggest themselves at once: all scholars acknowledge the great debt they owe to the editors, living and dead, of the MHSJ, a series in which so far ninety-three volumes have appeared.

tion of Peter Faber they were all laymen when they took their vows in 1534, accepting a certain leadership of Ignatius, their elder by more than ten years, and embracing a very uncertain future based upon a rather impractical promise to go to the Holy Land if they would find a ship in Venice to carry them there within the twelve months of 1537; if this plan failed, they would offer themselves to the pope.[3] And it is a strange type of prophet who, once the Society of Jesus has been founded, spends most of his life behind a desk writing a book of laws and numerous letters to keep a growing concern afloat. The success of this new foundation and its profound influence on the piety and spirituality of the Church for centuries to come suggest more the mystic who organized than the prophet who brought God's message to God's people.

It is true that Ignatius suffered persecution; throughout the years that followed his conversion he was always a suspect. It began a few years after his return from the Holy Land when his first brush with the Inquisition took place in Alcalá, and as late as 1555, a year before his death, the Sorbonne was still causing trouble.[4] His enemies, however, never attacked him because he was a troublesome man, hurling warnings against the leaders of a corrupt Church and hurting them in the process: they were truly worried about his orthodoxy and hence subjected the Spiritual Exercises to close scrutiny, suspecting heresy behind the simple phrase and naive-sounding sentence. But persecution and suspicion may mark the prophet; they do not make the prophet.

---

[3] *Autobiography* 85-86. Ignatius was often urged by his companions to give them the story of his past; only most reluctantly he gave in, but even then the things he thought fit to communicate are brief and incomplete. They only cover his life until the beginnings of the Society he founded. The little work as dictated to Gonzalez de Cámara is published in *Fontes Narrativi de S. Ignatio de Loyola et de Societatis Initiis*, Vol. I, 323-507 (Rome, 1943). In referring to this work we make use of the numbering of paragraphs as given in this edition.

[4] In his autobiography, Ignatius tells of his troubles in Alcalá (58-63), in Salamanca (64-70), in Paris (81, 86), in Venice (93) and in Rome (97). Cf. his letter to King Juan of Portugal, dated Rome, March 15, 1545 (*Fontes Narrativi* I, 51-54).

So far we have been silent about the man who in the opinion of many, both friend and enemy, was called by God to battle that dangerous enemy, the Reformation, and to put an end to its triumphant march across Europe. Here is a challenge worthy of a prophet, and it is a challenge for which Ignatius has been waiting. Denouncing Protestants of whatever shade, he recalls the prophets of old turning against God's enemies—Egypt, Assur, Edom, Moab and the rest. Our commentary is that here again we have bad history and distortion of the facts. It does not now matter that a fighter is not the same as a prophet; what matters is that the Reformation in whatever form—Lutheranism, Calvinism, Anglicanism and so forth—only touched Ignatius lightly. There were rumblings of the Reformation when he studied in Paris (1528-1535), where Calvin arrived in 1528 and to which he returned in 1531, and there is evidence that Ignatius was somewhat worried about one of his fellow students by the name of Francis Xavier.[5] He was undoubtedly informed of the clashes with Protestants when his companions traveled to Venice via Basel and Constance.[6] Soon after his arrival in Rome he is aware that the Holy City is not just a city of holiness and truth.[7] And as the years move on, he is brought face to face with the Reformation more and more. It here suffices to draw the attention to the foundation of the German College in 1552, to the letters which he wrote the same year and again in 1555 asking the Jesuits in Italy to pray for Germany, England and "the countries in the North", and to the serious thought he gave to the

[5] G. Schurhammer Si, *Franz Xavier. Sein Leben und seine Zeit* (Freiburg, 1955), pp. 158-62.

[6] MHSJ, *Epistolae PP. Paschasii Broëtii, Claudii Jaji, Joannis Coduri et Simonis Rodericii* (Matriti, 1903), 470-474, and Polanco's *Vita Ignatii Loiolae et Rerum Societatis Jesu Historia* (Matriti, 1894), 55.

[7] In a letter to Didacus de Gouvea, dated November 23, 1538, Ignatius observes that many want to go to India, adding however that there is plenty of work to do in Rome, where "there are many who little like the light of truth and life within the Church." In his opinion doctrinal errors proceed from errors in their way of living (*Ep.* I, 133). The twelve volumes of Ignatius' letters have been published in MHSJ, *Monumenta Ignatiana, Series prima* (Matriti, 1903-1911). The letters will be referred to as *Ep.*, followed by a Roman numeral indicating the volume.

establishment of colleges in Germany, especially in Cologne,[8] while the names of Faber and Canisius stand for his concern about Germany.

But even with such and similar facts before us, the Reformation must be said to have only brushed his cassock. Reading the instructions to Laynez, Le Jay and Salmerón who were going to the Council of Trent, one wonders whether the advice they contain is meant for great theologians attending a crucial council, or for zealous Christians, delegates to some meeting to further the aggiornamento of the Church (Ep. 1, 386-389). In the Constitutions, which for the greater part were written in the second half of the fifth decade, at the time therefore of the first sessions of the Council, the Reformation is hardly mentioned, let alone the fact that combating heresy is their inspiration. No matter whether Ignatius is dealing with the various works of his young Society, whether he is explaining how the scholastic should be formed, or whether he is laying down which subjects have to be taught in colleges and universities or which books to be stocked in the libraries, the Reformation does not really put in an appearance.[9] If we read the Formula Instituti, drawn up by Ignatius and made part of the Bulls of approbation of the Society of Jesus, or if we carefully study the various Bulls themselves, there might just as well have been no Reformation.[10] In the so called Deliberatio Primorum Patrum, which contains the discussions of

[8] *Ep.* V, 221; VIII, 266; a letter to the Carthusian monk Kalckbrenner dealing with the question of a college in Cologne is found in *Ep.* VIII, 583-585. The letter is dated March 22, 1555; on that same day a letter was written to the Senate of Nijmegen, Canisius' birthplace, and its subject is the foundation of a college there (*ibid.,* 585).

[9] Cf. IV, *prooemium,* and A, VII, c. 1, n. 1 and B, VII, c. 4, n. 3; IX, c. 3, n. 9, F; IV, c. 5, n. 1; IV, c. 12, nn. 2-3; IV, c. 7, n. 1; IV, c. 14, n. 1, A.

[10] In the Formula Instituti the Lutherans are mentioned, only to disappear in the Bull *Regimini militantis* (MHSJ, *Const.* I, 17, 27). Schismatics and heretics are found in the same Bull as well as in *Exposcit debitum,* but in these identical passages they are in the company of Turks and Indians and also of *quosvis fideles,* of all believers (*ibid.,* 28, 378). In the second Bull of Paul III, *Sacrosancte Romane Ecclesie* (1541), and in his third, *Iniunctum nobis* (1543), schismatics and heretics have disappeared, although the poor Turks are still there (*ibid.,* 70-77, 81-86).

Ignatius and his first companions about their future plans, as well as in other documents that precede the drawing up of the Constitutions, the Reformation plays no part.[11] We come across the *fieles y infieles,* believers and unbelievers, quite often in company with the people living in Turkey and India,[12] but that surely is not enough to justify looking upon Ignatius as a prophet who heard the challenge of the Reformation and took it up.

Even the story of colleges and universities thrown up like barricades to save Europe from the onrush of Protestantism is a myth. The first college, in far away Goa, the second in Alcalá, the third in Messina, are by their very location not bulwarks against an oncoming tide of false doctrines. Indeed, in the rules for thinking with the Church in the book of the Sp. Ex., mention is made of certain tenets that are closely associated with the Reformation, but this is done in an indirect, positive way. It is a question of recommending obedience to the Church, the reception of confession and communion, divine office, religious life, veneration of saints and relics, and so forth. Where doctrine is mentioned, Ignatius only warns to be careful when words like predestination or expressions such as faith informed by charity, grace and nature are being used. The noteworthy thing is that Ignatius is very mild and gentle in these rules, although he does speak of "in temporibus nostris tam periculosis" (369). But, however dangerous the times, meekness and humility dominate, not threats, and this holds good also of Constitutions and letters, and evidently Ignatius imparted this gentleness to his first companions.[13]

[11] When Ignatius and his first companions discussed where possibly the pope might send them, they speak of "indi, sive heretici sive alii quicumque fideles vel infideles" (MHSJ, *Const.* I, 3). In early drafts of the Constitutions, only the expression "entre fieles o entre infieles" (among believers or unbelievers) occurs (*ibid.,* 159-160).

[12] Cf., e.g., in documents preparatory to the Constitutions (MHSJ, *Const.* I, 10, 11), in the Formula Instituti (*ibid.,* 15, 17), in *Iniunctum nobis* (*ibid.,* 83) and even in a letter to Charles V (*ibid.,* 241). "Believers and unbelievers" is also found in the opening paragraph of the seventh part of the Constitutions (cf. previous note and also VII, c. 2, n. 1, F; VII, c. 4, n. 3; IX, c. 3, n. 9, F).

[13] In the Bull *Licet debitum* of Paul III (1549), permission is granted to

To give what we have said so far some deeper relief, we wish to point out that according to the Constitutions, Ignatius' main concern was *iuvare animas,* to help souls.[14] Among the many people he wished to help, a very important place is given to the *niños y rudes,* to children and unlettered people. A newly appointed rector (IV, c. 10, n. 10), the scholastic at the beginning and at the end of his formation (V, c. 1, n. 3: Ex. Gen. IV, 14), the fathers who teach in Ferrara, Florence, Naples and Modena (Ep. III, 542)—they shall all go to the children and uneducated people to teach them the catechism, and it is this group that is mentioned first when, in the introductory remarks to the Spiritual Exercises, Ignatius comes to speak of "those who receive the exercises" (18).[15] In a similar way the sick and the poor push their way forward in Ignatius' writings, and all Jesuits should always find out where the hospitals and the prisons are, and there share the hardships of their unfortunate fellow men.[16]

---

live "in the land of those excommunicated, heretics, schismatics or unbelievers" and "to converse with them" (notice that "converse", *conversari,* is used, not *disputari;* MHSJ, *Const.* I, 363), and Julius III urges the fathers of the Society to work for the reconciliation of those who are of other opinions (*dissidentium reconciliatio; ibid.,* 376). Cf. Ignatius' letter to Peter Canisius dated Rome, August 13, 1554, his instructions to those who were to depart for Germany and to those who were working in Ferrara, Florence, Naples and Modena (*Ep.* VII, 398-404; *Ep.* XII, 239-247; *Ep.* III, 545-546, 549). Polanco appears to have only pleasant memories of his encounter with Lutherans when he and his companions traveled from Paris to Venice: "They showed so much kindness," he comments (*op. cit.,* 55). The exception confirming the rule is found in the harsh words of Nadal when he defends Ignatius and his Spiritual Exercises against the criticism of Thomas Pedroche (Fontes Narrativi, I, 322).

[14] Cf. I, c. 2, n. 8; IV *prooemium* and c. 12, n. 1; X, n. 2. Vague expressions such as "to work faithfully in the vineyard of the Lord" and "works of charity", which occur frequently when the works of the Society are mentioned, underline the wide scope of Ignatius' foundation (cf., e.g., MHSJ, *Const.* I, 6, 15, 16, 25, 374).

[15] A special vow to devote themselves to this work is dealt with in the fifth part (c. 3, n. 3, B; 6, c. 4, n. 2). The *niños y rudes* are found in the various Bulls of approbation, and even in Ignatius' letter to Charles V they are not forgotten (MHSJ, *Const.* I, 10, 16, 18, 25, 26, 71, 241, 374, and so forth).

[16] The fathers sent to various places in Italy (*Ep.* III, 549) are told to visit hospitals and prisons, and those sent to Germany in 1549 are asked not to forget the sick and the prisoners or the *niños y rudes* (*Ep.* XII,

Equally clear as the inescapable obligations of going to the poor, the sick, the prisoners, and so forth are Ignatius' very urgent reminders that the members of his Society are a useless lot if they do not go to the people as *edifying men*. It is not even true doctrine that they have to place before men, women and children in the first place, but a good example. In Constitutions and letters, edification takes pride of place.[17]

It is here that we begin to discern the contours of a true prophet. To understand this, one must resolutely drop any idea of the prophet as a man preaching doom and gloom, announcing disasters to come. No prophet is a man wagging, as has been said, an incriminatory finger at the past and at the present, himself walking all the time backward into the future. More often than not, a prophet is first and foremost a man broken-hearted because of the state of the virgin Israel (Jer. 13, 17). Rebuilding walls (Jer. 31, 4) is more the prophet's task than fulminating against the enemy outside. When St. Paul speaks of prophecy, he uses the very word *aedificatio,* the building up of the Church (1 Cor. 14, 3-5. 12-26). It is the love for the People of God that moves the prophet; it is the love for the Church—especially when covered with wounds, often of her own making, that stirs the prophet.

In the case of Ignatius it is almost unbelievable how a man who had such a close look at what was taking place in the

243). The work among the sick is mentioned in the Formula Instituti (MHSJ, *Const.* I, 15, 19; one of the reasons why Ignatius did not want to see the members of the Society tied down to the divine office in choir is that they might have their hands free to attend the sick), in the Bull *Regimini militantis* and in the Bull *Exposcit debitum* (*ibid.*, 25, 376). According to the Constitutions all members of the Society shall devote themselves to the poor, the sick and those in prison (VII, c. 4, n. 9), while part of the formation of the young Jesuit is to spend at least a month serving the sick in hospitals (*Ex. Gen.* IV, n. 11, 16). And as if the fathers sent to the Council of Trent have nothing else to do or worry about, they are told not to omit visiting the sick and comforting the poor, and this every day (*Ep.* I, 387-388).

[17] Cf., e.g., VI, c. 2, n. 16; VII, c. 4, n. 2, 6; also IV, c. 10, n. 4; IX, c. 6, n. 1; X, n. 2. See the advice given to the fathers at Trent, to those sent to Germany and to those working in Italy (*Ep.* I, 386-388; XII, 243; III, 543, 545).

Church, from the papal court and the curia down to the most insignificant parish, who saw before his eyes that corruption was eating its way into her life, could still write of the *nuestra sancta madre Iglesia hierárchica* and the *vera sposa de Christo nuestro Señor* (Sp. Ex. 353). When Marcellus II was elected pope, a little more than a year before Ignatius' death and a little less than a month before his own death, Ignatius' joy is almost unbounded, because Marcellus is such a good man who from the very beginning meant business, doing away with abuses and scandals; the letter which he writes to his Society shows only too well how much he is aware of and suffers from the weakness and the wounds of the Church.[18]

Grief because of Israel, the old and the new, will move the prophet, but it is his vision and the message, spoken in Yahweh's name, that really make him so. It is not the evident sign of corruption that causes the tears; the sorrow finds its origin in the cause of the decay: the idols have ousted the true and living God. People have forsaken him who is the source of living waters and have forgotten him and his law (Jer. 2, 13; 9, 12; 18, 15; 19, 4); they do not know him (Jer. 9, 2), there is no longer any knowledge in the land (Hos. 4, 2. 6); it is the old, old story of the ox knowing its master and the donkey knowing the place where it can find its fodder, but Israel not knowing Yahweh (Is. 1, 3), so much so that the distinguishing feature of the New Covenant will be the knowledge of Yahweh throughout the land, a knowledge taught by Yahweh himself (Jer. 31, 34). Yahweh, who finds himself placed outside or at the periphery of his own people, is

---

[18] On April 10, 1555, Ignatius' secretary Polanco writes to Father Araoz, a nephew of Ignatius and provincial in Spain, that the newly elected pope is "a man of great integrity and ardent zeal for the reformation of the Church"; he has begun his pontificate by refusing any favors to those who were present at the conclave, by not confirming concessions given by his predecessors to cardinals until they have been carefully examined, and by abolishing the lavish and expensive feasts of election and coronation (*Ep.* VIII, 665-666). Four days later Ignatius writes a letter to all members of the Society praising the new pope for the measures he has taken, mostly directed against waste of money, nepotism, slackness in spiritual matters, and so on (*Ep.* IX, 13-17). Two weeks later Marcellus II died (April 30).

the inspiration of true prophecy; hence, in the end, the essence of the prophet's message will be none other than: "In your midst stands he whom you do not know" (Jn. 1, 26).

At this point we must turn to the Spiritual Exercises, which are the fruit of Ignatius' profound spiritual experiences at Manresa. We do not discuss the question whether or not the election of a state or way of life is the purpose of the Exercises; [19] we observe that from the early beginnings, strictly according to the text from the third day onward, the knowledge of the Lord is the heart of everything. In the first contemplation of the second week the exercitant is moved by the desire to know the Lord better in order to love him more and serve him more faithfully (104), and it should be remembered that this first contemplation is given as a model of all the contemplations of the second week (131). This desire to know the Lord more and the prayer inspired by it find their origin in the conviction that God has been ousted by his own creatures, who have now become as blind men (102, 106, 107). A newly regained knowledge and love of the Lord will lead to sharing both the sufferings and the joys of Christ crucified but risen (193, 203, 221) and will find its climax in the vision and experience of God in all things (233-237). One must not overlook that the Sp.Ex. are not a kind of closed circuit which it takes thirty days to cover; the retreat is a time of prayer but also a school of prayer, and so the desire to know the Lord better will remain with the exercitant in the weeks and months and years to come (162, 262).

The knowledge of the Lord is imparted by God; it is God's gift, not the result of man's own efforts or studies, even less of the retreat master's sermons or conferences (2). God enlightens, God communicates, God moves and stirs, God gives peace and comfort, and so forth (2, 15, 16, 316, 329, 330, 336). All the time God is teaching the exercitant as a schoolmaster teaches the child, as Ignatius confessed with regard to his own experiences at

[19] The reader is referred to W. Peters, *The Spiritual Exercises of St. Ignatius. Exposition and Interpretation* (Jersey City, 1968).

Manresa (Autobiography 27). We stress this activity of God because the astounding thing is that it is to be part and parcel of the prophet's message.

Even this early in our exposition of Ignatius as a prophet, we have evidently moved far away from anything that is associated with the Reformation, and even with disruptive forces within the Church. The prophet's gaze is turned toward God, unknown, much forgotten, little loved, who wants to reveal himself and communicate himself (15). Here both friend and enemy will be very anxious to know what kind of God this prophet will bring to the people. If there has been much controversy about Ignatius during the past four centuries, it has in no small measure been caused by a—for many—unacceptable presentation of who and what God is.

There can be no doubt that the vision Ignatius received when one day during his stay at Manresa he was looking down at the waters of the Cardoner was the greatest mystical gift of his life: he himself clearly indicates this in his autobiography (32). Its contents and importance has been brilliantly analysed in one of Hugo Rahner's finest essays.[20] For the purpose of this article it suffices to observe that the exercise "to attain the love of God" (230-237), a clear echo of which is found in Ignatius' treatment of the general examination of conscience (40) as well as in many a letter,[21] is the direct fruit of this vision. In this contemplation the exercitant experiences the presence throughout creation of the Blessed Trinity as a God of love. Creation is seen to be the work, not the product, of a loving God, always toiling, always giving, and always hoping that his gifts of love will move the exercitant to a response of love. The whole of creation be-

[20] H. Rahner, "Die Vision des H. Ignatius in der Kapelle von La Storta," in *Zeitschr. f. Aszese u. Mystik* 10 (1935), pp. 17-35, 124-39, 202-20, 265-89. Cf. H. Rahner, *Ignatius von Loyola als Mensch und Theologe* (Freiburg, 1963), pp. 53-108, esp. pp. 80-87.

[21] To confine ourselves to three clear instances: Ignatius' letter to his sister Magdalena dated Rome, May 24, 1541, to Francis Borgia toward the end of 1545, and to Father Brandano on June 1, 1551 (*Ep.* I, 170-171; *ibid.*, 339-342; *Ep.* III, 506-513).

comes transparent so that man comes to see, experience and love God in all things (233, 235, 236) and all things in God (237, 316).

One should realize that *Dios nuestro Señor* stands for the Blessed Trinity. He is not only creator, redeemer and lover,[22] but as this contemplation follows upon the contemplations of the second, third and fourth weeks, the Blessed Trinity necessarily and very distinctly recalls the Father who sent his Son into this world (102, 108, 109). This implies that the exercitant finds himself face to face with the Father sending his Son into this world that he might win back the love of mankind which in its blindness had left no place for him in its midst (102, 107)—the Father who forsook his Son on the cross, making him sin (2 Cor. 5, 21), but also gave him a name that is above every other name (Phil. 2, 9). It also implies that the exercitant is face to face with Christ who became obedient unto death, and whose death is the very source of life, first to himself and then to all who become like him in death (Rom. 6, 4; 8, 11; Phil. 3, 10). For Ignatius the risen Christ is always Christ crucified, and risen because crucified. In the Spiritual Exercises there is no break between the end of the third week and the beginning of the fourth week, between Good Friday and Easter Sunday.[23] And the wounds are still there to show how only love—that is, the Holy Spirit, explains what reality exactly means.

Where the vision of this prophet is his message, Ignatius shouts from the housetops that the God whom we do not know is the Father who has revealed himself in his Son, crucified but alive and now fulfilling his task of comforter (224) within creation, within this world, within the human family. God is no sovereign being existing outside the work of his hands: as Emmanuel and

[22] In the first point of the contemplation, Ignatius writes of the gifts of being created and redeemed, while "to give oneself" is the proof and expression of love (233, 231). Cf. the fourth note of the fourth week, in which "creator and redeemer" does not refer to Christ but to the Blessed Trinity (229); *see* W. Peters. *op. cit.,* pp. 149-51.

[23] We refer once again to our study of the Spiritual Exercises mentioned above, especially chapter 13.

love he is in our very midst, and it is there that man shall find
and experience and love him.

True prophecy goes hand in hand with a right understanding
of the signs of the times. As a prophet with this message, Ignatius
stands at the beginning of our modern era which has pushed God
more and more to the periphery of the universe and of man's
existence. How badly mistaken modern man has been—and still
is—in this matter.

Ignatius does not stop here. The visionary, the mystic and the
prophet has no choice but to proclaim boldly that God is present
and works in and through his creatures not in a vague general
sort of way; it is above all in man that this mystery is realized. As
Lord, God will order man's life, dispose it, dispose of it and
make use of it (Ex. Sp. 5, 15, 234). Man is destined to be God's
instrument, but as man is endowed with free will, this always
implies the free cooperation of man (15); it is man's duty to see
that he is closely joined to him who handles him as his instrument. This conviction is clearly expressed in the Constitutions
and in many a letter.[24]

Possibly we are not entirely happy with this idea of instru-
mentality; it suggests a contact with God that is mechanical and
rather impersonal. In the tenth part of the Constitution, however, where we find the clearest expression of Ignatius' vision, he
goes on to stress that such instrumental use of man is primarily
based upon the closest personal union with God, in which connection he even speaks of familiarity with God in one's spiritual
exercises, a phrase that reminds one of what Ignatius looks for
above all other things in the general of his Society—namely, that
he be a man *cum Deo ac Domino nostro quam maxime con-
junctus et familiaris* (IX, c. 2, n. 1). Nor must it be forgotten that
in Ignatius' vision man himself is God's image and his temple (Sp.

[24] The *locus classicus* is found in the Constitutions (X, n. 2, 3). As re-
gards this conviction expressed in his letters, to mention a few, see one
written to the fathers in Louvain and Cologne (*Ep.* II, 285), to Francis
Xavier (*Ep.* IV, 128), to Francis Borgia (*Ep.* VII, 111; VIII, 198), to
Nadal (*Ep.* VII, 139), to Miron (*Ep.* IV, 561-562) and Caspar Berze
(*Ep.* VI, 87).

Ex. 235), in whom he lives, in whom he works (235, 236) and
to whom he desires to give himself as much as possible (234), so
much so that he not only surrounds man with all sorts of created
things (enumerated in the second Exercise: 60) but makes man
share in his justice, goodness, mercy and so forth. As the waters
of the source are the waters of the river, so do we find the waters
of God's infinite perfections in the perfections of man. Ignatius
does not use the word "incarnation" in this connection, but it is
clear that in his vision God's wisdom, patience, gentleness and so
forth find a home in man. It is not surprising that, although man
is God's instrument, he is this in such a manner that he is truly
Lord of creation at the same time, whom all creatures help and
serve (23, 60).

Once again, we are reminded how this prophet read the signs
of his times and of time to come. The Renaissance preached and
practiced that man was coming into his own, and he made himself the center and master of whatever he observed, just as man
nowadays considers himself as having reached adulthood and
hence can decide for himself what to do and how to think and
act. With certain reservations all this is acceptable. The danger
and temptation, however, is that man, then and now, forgets that
the God in our midst remains the Señor, the Dominus. This is the
key word of the Spiritual Exercises, of the Constitutions and of
the letters of Ignatius.[25]

Ignatius' vision of the way in which universe, man and God
are inextricably joined together, and his conviction that God
who is always present and always working in all things cannot do
without man's cooperation, explain what almost amounts to his
obsession of seeking and finding the will of God (Sp. Ex. 1, 5,
15, 91, 180, 234). In one of the earliest extant letters we already
come across what will be the normal closing phrase of by far the
greatest part of his letters—namely, a request for prayers that

---

[25] Outside the Exercise on the kingdom the word "king" does not occur;
in the meditation on the two standards Christ is only referred to as "Capi-
tán" in the preludes and in the introduction to the second part of the
Exercise (136, 138, 139 and 143). For Ignatius, Christ is "el Señor."

God may be good enough to make known his most holy will and may give the grace to fulfill it (Ep. I, 82). This request, so frequently repeated, suggests that it is no easy matter to discover the will of God. It not only presupposes a strong *devotio,* which Ignatius describes as the ease of finding God in all things (Autobiography 98), but also a great sensitivity enabling man to discern by what kind of spirit, conscious and subconscious, natural and supernatural, good or evil—and the latter making himself into an angel of light (2 Cor. 11, 14; Sp. Ex. 332)—he is being moved.

It is one of those incomprehensible twists in the history of the life of Ignatius that his name has become almost identical with structure, framework, rules, blind surrender and an inhuman sort of obedience, while in fact the poor man himself is worried to death to find God's will, which is always so much more than any structure or any rule, and can never be comprehended within these. Or again, it is very strange that his name has become linked with a reasoned, well-argued method of discovering the will of God by weighing pro's and cons, the so called third time (Sp. Ex. 178-188), while in fact he himself shows so little confidence in this method that he forbids using it when there is question of an immutable choice (178). Again, it seems difficult to understand that rigidity suggests itself as soon as the name of Ignatius is mentioned, while in fact his characteristic feature is to be open, to be at God's disposal, which implies the greatest inward mobility and flexibility.

The paradox that no doubt has misled people is that at the same time Ignatius stands for emotional and psychological stability. However, this does not clash with flexibility, but is its very foundation. The real difficulty is of course that God who moves and stirs, enlightens, communicates and comforts is not easily discernible; God's movements are so often beyond the emotional, even beyond what we consciously experience. His movements made Ignatius think of a drop of water that falls on a sponge, not causing any splash (Sp. Ex. 335), and for man who tends to equate reality with what he observes by the senses or consciously experiences, the temptation to conclude that nothing happens is frequently too great to resist.

It is only one of the many paradoxes that Ignatius presents when we see him as he is: a true prophet. From the somewhat misty surroundings of the Renaissance and the Reformation and the confusion of our own times, he comes to us not as one whose prophecy is his preaching, or his writing, or his way of life, but as a man sent by God to be a prophet by his approach to reality and his vision and grip of its totality. This is always a question of *and—and,* never of *either—or.* He was a leader and organizer, and at the same time a man almost immoderately given to tears so that his eyesight suffered badly.[26] He was a man passionately in love with created things, yet placing himself at a distance lest they should master instead of serve him (23). The profane did not exist for him; things were only sacred because God was seen to be present and to be working within them. He acknowledged that man was God's instrument, and at the same time knew that the faithful servant was lord of creation. He was in need of redemption but also called to cooperate in God's redemptive work of all mankind. He wept because of Good Friday and rejoiced because of Easter Sunday, and in his mystical experience both were present now, and not past. He lived in a world which had become truly transparent, and so he could mix the serious and a lovely sense of humor (Ep. VI, 357-359), profound insight into God's mysteries and sound common sense and an endearing wisdom (Ep. I, 495-510; XII, 151-152). For him there was no clash between faith and reason, between grace and nature (Ep. II, 474-484; IX, 626-627). The breathing man was the praying man (Sp. Ex. 258-260).

[26] Abundant evidence is found in what is usually called Ignatius' diary. It contains, however, no more than two sets of notes, sometimes very brief, all of them dealing with his spiritual experiences during the periods of February 2 to March 12, 1544 (Ignatius at this time is wrestling with the problem of poverty in his Society) and March 13, 1544 to February 27, 1545 (MHSJ, *Const.* I, 86-158).

Ignatius is a man *composed;* this is the result of composition, a word frequently used in the Spiritual Exercises; every Exercise begins with an act of composing oneself. Its result is oneness, harmony and order. Composition is the essence of Ignatius' message as it is the heart of his vision of creator and creation. We do well to listen to this prophet in a time when the world we live in is anything but a world composed and ordered, but very much a splintered world, and man himself is being cut into pieces by the anthropologist, the sociologist and the psychologist, not to mention the politician, the businessman and the bureaucrat, when he is liable to be reduced to a being with five senses, three faculties, and many known and unknown, conscious and unconscious tendencies. To this we have to add that the Church is rather a splintered Church, in which dogma, liturgy, piety, asceticism, Canon Law and exegesis to a large extent lead their own independent existence. The prophet Ignatius does not merely take his stand against so much disorder; he clearly shows whence this disorder proceeds, and indicates the way we have to go in order to overcome it. His message concerns the God who stands in our very midst, yet whom we do not know. There is a crying need today that modern man hears and listens to this message.

Gordon Rupp/*Cambridge, England*

John Wesley: Christian Prophet

The life of John Wesley (born: June 17, 1703 in Epworth; died March 2, 1791 in London) and the emergence of the people called Methodists (his name for his followers) raise questions of current ecumenical importance, not least that of the missionary apostolate of the whole Church, and of the sovereign liberty of the Holy Spirit to work *ubi et quando* he may choose, sometimes in those extraordinary ministries and movements of which John Wesley and the Evangelical Revival are striking examples.

John Wesley, the neat, trim little parson who could halt a service in the open air while they fetched his cassock, the stickler for punctuality to whom untidiness, whether mental or physical, was an affront, and whose self-discipline was always more austere than anything he demanded of his followers, does not fit the common image of a prophet, whether of the Old or New Dispensation. He has almost nothing in common with that other John, the Baptist, save perhaps that he too was "a man sent from God to bear witness to the Light".

Certainly he was no seer, in the manner of a Joachim da Fiore, nor do his writings abound in premonitions of a coming age, as do those of Newman. "One-sided? When has a prophet not been one-sided?" asked Hans Lietzmann at the close of a famous essay on Marcion which many took to be a covert de-

scription of the young Karl Barth. For that lopsidedness of theological genius which can plunge deep beneath the surface of an
age, the genius of a Tertullian, an Abelard or a Kierkegaard,
John Wesley had no facility. And though a reading of his works
would be rewarding today since the cast of his mind (typified in
the title of his "appeal to men of reason and religion") is an
antidote to our current flight from reason, and though a tired
and feverish contemporary Protestantism is more than in need of
a renewal of what Wesley called "inward religion", "Wesley
says" is not likely to have the talismanic aura which is accorded
to the *obiter dicta* of Luther or the pronouncements of John
Calvin.

The Spiritual Inheritance

God makes ready the ways of his servants, the prophets, and it
is important to glance at the background and training of John
Wesley. As it took generations of musicians in the Bach family to
produce John Sebastian, so John Wesley came of four generations of clergy in the Church of England. In his home there was a
blending of two great strains of English spirituality, which in the
17th century had been locked in conflict, that of Puritanism, and
that of the High Anglican, Arminian piety. Grandfather Bar-
tholomew and great-grandfather John Wesley had been among
the ejected Puritan clergy, and John Wesley must often have
been told of their forthrightness and courage, their bearing under
persecution, their strong sense that where the Spirit is, there must
be liberty. When, later, he came to give his followers that astonishing collection of *lectio divina,* his "Christian Library" in 52
volumes, culled from all levels of spiritual and practical divinity,
Puritan writings were the chief single source.

On the other hand, both his parents were converts from dis-
sent. His mother, the incomparable Susanna, was a Non-Juror,
and his father, the redoubtable Samuel, a High Church "Con-
vocation Man". Despite the problem of rearing a score of children, many of whom died in infancy, she took pains with the
religion of her children until she could discuss learnedly and with

insight the writings of B. Pascal with her undergraduate son. Samuel was a formidable example of stubborn if tactless faithfulness, and his letter "To a Curate" includes a vast program of patristic studies which reflects the best High Church traditions of his generation. Through him John Wesley learned to read the Fathers, and when he came to draw up his "Christian Library", the writings of Macarius would be in the forefront. He also had a high regard for the works of Ephraem Syrus. It is no wonder then, that his intimates at Oxford, particularly those in the strictly disciplined "Holy Club", were High Churchmen and Non-Jurors.

"Inward Religion" in the 18th Century

Through them he came in touch with that remarkable movement, lately traced for us by Professor Orcibal,[1] almost an abortive ecumenical movement, an international traffic in spiritual theology, at the heart of which stood the Non-Jurors with their interest in the primitive Church and in liturgical studies, and who now made available in English the minor classics of Spanish, Italian and French mysticism and some of the treatises of the Jansenists. In this way, John Wesley came to have a considerable knowledge of Catholic literature. It is true that this was a little one-sided, for it gave prominence to Fenelon, Mme. Guyon and Antoinette Bourignon rather than Theresa and John of the Cross. The Catholics whom John Wesley rated but little lower than the angels were the Mexican hermit, Gregory Lopez, and the French nobleman, M. de Renty. Of deep and immediate impact on him in his Oxford days were *Holy Living and Holy Dying* by the Anglican divine, Bishop Jeremy Taylor, *Serious Call to a Devout and Holy Life* by his Non-Juror mentor, William Law, and above all that classic of modern devotion, *The Imitation of Christ* which he later abridged for the Methodists and often republished under the title *The Christian Pattern*. Here he found a call to seek for evangelical perfection through prayer

---

[1] J. Orcibal, "The Spirituality of John Wesley," in *A History of the Methodist Church in Great Britain,* ed. Rupp and Davies (1965).

and discipline, and this was the program by which he and his companions in the Holy Club sought to recapture the spirit and piety of primitive Christianity.

John Wesley as Missionary

There followed the abortive mission of John Wesley and his younger brother Charles to the Red Indians in the outpost of the British Empire, in the colony of Georgia. It ended in bitter disappointment for John Wesley and in near disgrace for Charles. Their naive sincerities were entangled in a network of evil devices (for which a sheltered upbringing had but ill prepared them), and gossip and malicious invention disastrously broke their personal relations with the governor, General Oglethorpe. John Wesley's poignant but entirely honorable love affair with the young Sophy Hopkey brought him into conflict with her uncle, the local magistrate in Savannah. More important was his failure to impress the very mixed community in the colony of transported debtors, exiled Presbyterians and emigrant Lutherans. He attempted to impose upon them the strict rubrics of High Churchmen, the First Prayer Book of Edward VI, and the discipline of a Holy Club. And when they grumbled at this unheard-of brand of religion, which was neither Catholic fish, nor Protestant fowl, nor Anglican good red herring, he could not tell them that here, in Georgia, was Methodism in embryo. "The circuit, the society, the itinerant ministry, the class meeting, the band meeting, the love feast, leaders and lay assistants, ex tempore preaching and prayer—all this . . . of early Methodism came to John Wesley in Georgia." [2]

Through Humiliation to Justification

To this we must add that this experience of personal humiliation and failure is an important ingredient in the formation of John Wesley's character and ministry, and he was nearer to salvation than he knew when he cried on the return voyage: "I went to America to convert the Indians, but oh, who shall con-

[2] *The Journal of John Wesley*, ed. N. Curnock (1938), Vol. 1, p. 426.

vert me?" There was another powerful instrument at work in his mind, and this not so much from books, as through his personal contact with the Moravians, and through them with the powerful movement in Lutheran Germany of Pietism. Through them he learned that true, saving faith comes when we renounce trust in our own virtues and cast ourselves on the mercy declared to men in Christ. It is no accident that it should be his reading of Luther's *Preface to the Romans* that the Word of God struck in his heart that fire which had been the apt metaphor of Pascal's great experience. Now he was not content simply to admire the Moravians, to listen to them and to translate German hymns. In 1738 he made an important trip to Germany "to see where the Christians live", as he told an astonished Saxon customs officer. Here he saw the great philanthropic institutions of the German renewal, the schools in Jena, and the orphanage at Halle. But here above all he saw in the Moravian settlement at Herrenhuth a marvelous and intricate system of corporate faith and worship, wheels within wheels, some small, some great, of companies of disciplined Christians. He never forgot what he saw on that memorable visit, and most of it he copied in the institutions of Methodism.

And now, on the very edge of the greatest missionary apostolate in British history, there came, at the last moment, a setback. Wesley and his friends were already at work in little religious societies, preaching and teaching among them in London and elsewhere. But that autumn of 1738, one by one the doors of the fashionable churches were closed on them. Time after time, Wesley records in his journal that he is to preach in that particular church no more.

The Beginnings of the Evangelical Revival

Modern historians set the work of the Wesley brothers in wider perspective. The Evangelical Revival has been shown to have been much wider: already before the "evangelical conversion" of John and Charles Wesley, movements of renewal had begun in America and in Wales. A series of biographies in the last decades have delineated the Anglican Evangelicals, large numbers of clergy keeping within the discipline of the Church of England, men of evangelical zeal and pastoral care which brought a harvest of converted souls—men like Walker in Cornwall and Grimshaw in Yorkshire.

On this, two comments should be made. The first is that these men were in the main Calvinist in their theology. The High Church legacy in John and Charles Wesley made them Arminians: not the abstract Arminianism of Dutch theology or the semi-Pelagianism of High Anglican Churchmanship, but what Methodists themselves called Evangelical Arminianism, the conviction that God offered salvation to all men, that "for all my Savior died," an optimism of grace confident that the very strongholds of evil could be overthrown, an emblem of which is Wesley's cry (August, 1777): "Give me one hundred preachers who fear nothing but sin and desire nothing but God and I care not a straw whether they be clergy or laymen; such alone will shake the gates of hell and set up the kingdom of heaven on earth." And the second difference consists in the men themselves, John and Charles Wesley. It is still true that without John Wesley the story of the Evangelical Revival in England would be Hamlet without the prince of Denmark.

We must not exaggerate the difference in effect between the Calvinist and the Evangelical Arminian preaching. The greatest preacher of them all was their Calvinist comrade George Whitefield. He it was who called John Wesley to preach in the open air: to go through the great door that now opened up as the church doors slammed in their faces.

Open-Air Preaching

Thus began the adventure of which the two notes in Wesley's Journal for 1739 (March 31 and April 1) are the memorial.

In the evening I reached Bristol and met Mr. Whitefield there. I could scarce reconcile myself at first to this strange way of preaching in the fields, of which he set me an example on Sunday: having all my life (till very lately) been so tenacious of every point relating to decency and order, that I should have thought the saving of souls almost a sin if it had not been done in church.

At four in the afternoon I submitted to be more vile, and proclaimed in the highways the glad tidings of salvation, speaking from a little eminence in a ground adjoining to the city to about three thousand people. The scripture on which I spoke was this: Is it possible anyone should be ignorant that it is fulfilled in every true minister of Christ? "The Spirit of the Lord is upon me because he hath anointed me to preach the Gospel to the poor. He hath sent me to heal the broken hearted; to preach deliverance to the captive and recovery of sight to the blind; to set at liberty them that are bruised, to proclaim the acceptable year." [3]

Now there opened up a series of endless audiences, eager and tumultuous, with Bristol, Newcastle and London as pivots, among the rough mining communities of Wales and Cornwall, the thronging villages of the new industrial areas, and the squalid, teeming heart of London itself. For in that age, the population had moved out and spilled across old boundaries, and an Established Church which must seek an act of parliament for each new parish it would create left many thousands of souls unchurched and without either the Word or sacraments. Wesley found helpers in a small band of ordained clergy of the Church of England and a growing company of lay preachers, men of coarse spiritual cloth, but strong, dedicated and fearless. He himself set the example in his tireless journeyings which took him 250,000 miles up and down the land. Like his great distant kinsman, the Duke of Wellington, he had the knack of turning up just where he was wanted, at the critical moment, and he seemed to be all over the place at once.

To preach with converting power, to touch the unchurched

[3] *Ibid.*, Vol. 2, pp. 167ff.

multitudes was but the beginning. Others did the same, but their converts melted away. "A rope of sand," sighed Wesley about Whitefield's followers. It was Wesley who adapted the Moravian machinery of pastoral care and made it missionary and dynamic; there was no Methodist Herrenhuth, though there were very soon Methodist schools and orphanages. For the Moravian monasticism, Wesley substituted something moving, such as had hardly been known since the coming of the friars. He had not so much a talent for organization as a genius for improvisation and adapting, and almost all the characteristic institutions of the Methodists are of this kind. In the first years, there were emotional scenes and what are often described but ill explained as "psychophysical phenomena". Yet, despite Msgr. Knox, the Methodist revival will not fit entirely within a compendium history of "enthusiasm" from Montanism to Pentecostalism. There was also fierce, cruel persecution from mobs and magistrates and sometimes from the clergy.

Economic historians have conceded the effect of the revival on manners and morals in whole communities where drunkenness disappeared and profligacy vanished, and among incredibly brutish sections of the people there appeared new, neat companies of sober, reliable, thrifty and hardworking, God-fearing citizens.

The New Wine and the Old Wineskins

But how did this new wine exist in the old wineskins? It is easy to number the growing points of tension between the Methodists and the Established Church within which Wesley intended firmly to keep his people. For many the Methodists represented an uncongenial religiosity, in an age deadly tired of the kind of "enthusiasm" which had filled the 17th century with ugly zeal, shouting and clamor. The preaching of a pleasant, worldly moralism had come to take the place of the vehement supernaturalisms of the preceding age. There were the stories, not always exaggerated, of quietism and antinomianism on the fringe, though not at the core of the new movement. Above all, there were the questions of the Methodist preachers themselves, and of John Wesley's own disregard of parochial boundaries. About this, however, he had made up his mind and declared himself in a famous letter even before the field preaching had begun. His letter to James Hervey (March 20, 1739) is almost a manifesto.

> You ask . . . : How is it that I assemble Christians who are none of my charge to sing psalms and pray and hear Scriptures expounded? And you think it hard to justify doing this in other men's parishes, upon Catholic principles.
>
> Permit me to speak plainly. If by Catholic principles you mean any other than scriptural they weight nothing with me. . . . God in Scripture commands me, according to my power, to instruct the ignorant, reform the wicked, confirm the virtuous. Man forbids me to do this in another's parish: that is, in effect not to do it at all. . . . Whom then shall I hear, God or man? If it be just to obey man rather than God, judge you. A dispensation of the Gospel is committed to me: and woe is me if I preach not the Gospel.
>
> Suffer me now to tell you my principles in this matter. I look upon all the world as my parish: thus far I mean that in whatever part of it I am, I judge it meet, right and my bounden duty to declare, unto all that are willing to hear, the glad tidings of salvation. This is the work which I know God has called me to: and sure I am that his blessing attends it.[4]

The same was true of the Methodist preachers. The classic definition of the scope of their work was set down in an early question addressed to them at their Conference.

Q.   How shall we look upon the Methodist preachers?

A.   As messengers raised up by the Lord, out of the common way, to provoke the regular clergy to jealousy,

[4] *The Letters of John Wesley*, ed. Telford (1931) Vol. 1., p. 285.

by supplying their lack of service toward those who are perishing for lack of knowledge, and above all to reform the nation, by spreading scriptural holiness throughout the land.

An Extraordinary Ministry?

Here, then, is a claim to be called by God, to an extraordinary ministry of evangelism and of building up men and women to salvation (for John Wesley claimed that the doctrine of perfect love was the grand depositum of Methodism for which God appeared to have chiefly raised them up).

But the Methodists had a double pattern of spirituality. There were the ordinances of the Church of England, of Word and sacraments. There was also the spiritual fabric of the Methodists, the intimate bands which were almost lay confessionals, the class meeting which was the essential cell, or koinonia, the love feasts and the occasional splendid eucharistic solemnities when thousands gathered at the Lord's table and when Wesley and his ordained Anglican friends administered. As far as was possible, the revival was sacramental, and we might say that with John Wesley the sacraments themselves became evangelical and therefore prophetic. They became, as he put it, "converting ordinances" where men might find their sins forgiven and the assurance of faith. The great saint of the Revival was Fletcher of Madeley, and in his age he was visited by two of the preachers. As they waited without, booted and spurred, beside their horses, he brought them out a tray on which were bread and wine. What might have been the normal courtesies of refreshment took another turn when Fletcher prayed the prayer of consecration and the three solemnly partook of body and of blood. Could there be a better emblem of the eschatological character of the eucharist and of the apostolic commission than these men, with the urgency of the Gospel written into their very riding habits?

Wesley himself distinguished clearly between the commission to preach and authority to administer the sacraments: the first he thought a prophetic office, the second to depend on ecclesiastical authority. He developed this in his sermon on "The Ministerial Office".[5] He affirms that in ancient times the office of a priest and that of a preacher were distinct—from Noah to Moses "the eldest of the family was the priest, but any other might be the prophet". So in the New Israel, in the early Church, "I do not find that ever the office of an Evangelist was the same with that of a pastor, frequently called a bishop. He presided over the flock and administered the sacraments". In this light, Wesley goes on, are the lay preachers of Methodism to be regarded. "We received them wholly and solely to preach, not to administer the sacraments. . . . In 1744 all the Methodist Preachers had their first Conference. But none of them dreamed that being called to preach gave them any right to administer sacraments."

Whatever we think of Wesley's strange view of sacred history in the matter of priests and prophets, and his sometimes eccentric exegesis, his distinction is important and deserves serious consideration, for it had important practical consequences. While he lived, the Methodists who acknowledged his authority did not permit laymen to administer the sacraments. To this day, in the Methodist Church the distinction holds good. Laymen may preach the Gospel, but they may not administer the sacraments. Only from time to time, under specific dispensation from the Conference, may they do so, where it can be shown that otherwise the faithful would be deprived of regular access to the sacraments. This was the overriding principle—that Christian people must have access to the Word and sacraments. It was the failure of the bishop of London, despite repeated petitions, to provide sufficient clergy for North America, and the ecclesiastical chaos caused by the War of Independence, which led Wesley in 1784 to ordain four clergymen for America, and in later years a handful of clergy for Scotland and England.

At the end of his life Wesley pondered the swift, deep extension of the revival to the very ends of the land. Though he did not live to see it, the great work was to be repeated in the next

[5] *The Works of the Rev. John Wesley M.A.*, ed. Jackson (1829), Vol. VII, pp. 273ff.

generation in North America, the West Indies, Africa, Australia and the islands of the Pacific. His own comment on it all was: "What hath God wrought!" and whether we take it affirmatively, or whether we turn it into a question mark, it is the question which John Wesley and his work ask of contemporary ecumenical theology.

Elisabeth Behr-Sigel/*Nancy, France*

The Russian "Startsy": Monks of "Holy Russia"

hanks to the novels of Dostoevski, the Russian *startsy* have made their appearance on the spiritual horizon of the West, and it is therefore not surprising that, as Zosima in *The Brothers Karamazov* and as Tychon in *The Possessed,* they have come to be considered as typical representatives of a specifically Slavic spirituality (we leave aside the vexed question of the writer's historical model or the poetic image's fidelity to the original). As a consequence, we have already been able to obtain a picture of the "starets" from hagiographic documents, while at the same time discovering an authentic creation of the religious genius of Christian Russia and a typical expression of the Russian "idea" of the "holy monk".[1]

Even so, this originality should not make us forget that Russian Christianity has its roots in the spiritual soil of Orthodoxy as a whole. As a result, the Russian *startsy* of the 19th century seem to be heirs to an uninterrupted monastic tradition (despite temporary eclipses) which was transmitted to Russia by Byzantium and periodically restored and renovated, and which dated back to the desert fathers of the first centuries of Christianity and, perhaps, even as far back as the "hassidim" [2] of biblical times.

[1] E. Behr-Sigel, *Prière et Sainteté dans l'Eglise Russe* (Paris, 1950), pp. 129-40.

[2] L. Gillet, "Note sur le mot 'Saint'," in *Contacts* 37 (1962), p. 20.

Moreover, to the orthodox theologian this *continuity-diversity* of charismatics is the historical expression of an essential principle fundamental to the scheme of salvation: the action of the Spirit, distinct from and yet indissolubly linked to the work of the Son, in the life of the Church.[3]

Seen in this wider perspective, the typical image of the Russian *starets* would be that of a local variant, at a given time in the history of the Church of an archetype that is truly Catholic (in a qualitative as well as a spatial sense of the term) and of an idea that was present in the Christian consciousness from the beginnings. Receiving its true light from the revelation of the Trinity, its forms were constantly renovated by the Spirit and testified to the eternal vigor of the evangelical message.

Origins and Genesis of the Monastic Spiritual Paternity

The etymological meaning of the Slavonic word *starets* is "the elder", the "old man", with a nuance of respect and deference. In its monastic usage, the word has a more precise sense and assumes a new significance. A *starets* is not necessarily an aged man. He is an adult Christian—i.e., someone who has reached inner maturity thanks to the gift of the Spirit. Once he has become "spiritual", he is able to initiate others into the life of the Spirit and to guide them along the path of monastic asceticism and prayer.

Using the word in this sense, the Slavic *starets* is the equivalent of the Greek *pater pneumatikos,* of whom both the idea and the reality were apparent in the primitive monachism of the desert fathers. Spiritual paternity, as practiced in this milieu and later in Byzantine and Russian monachism, did not depend on age or on any sacerdotal function but on personal charisma. As we may read in the *Apophtegmata Patrum:*

"One day, Abba Moses said to brother Zacariah: 'Tell me what I must do.' At these words, the latter threw himself at the feet of the old man and said: 'Is it I that you are questioning,

---

[3] V. Lossky, *Essai sur la théologie mystique de l'Eglise d'Orient* (Paris, 1944), pp. 171ff.

Father?' The old man said to him: 'Believe me, Zacariah, I have seen the Holy Ghost descend upon you and since then I am obliged to question you.' " [4]

Similarly, Simeon the New Theologian affirmed: "He who is not yet engendered is not able to engender his spiritual children. ... To give the Spirit, one must have it."

According to this "desert" tradition to which the whole of Orthodox monachism has made ceaseless reference, the spiritual father may be a layman as was Antony, the founder of monachism. A simple monk, the *pater pneumatikos,* is qualified to hear confessions—a fact also admitted by the Patriarch Nicephorus and Simeon the New Theologian.[5] Only later did the Church reserve the right to give absolution to the priest alone. It should also be added that from the time of this "desert" monachism, spiritual paternity has sometimes been extended to Christians living in the world, but this universality was to become most strikingly apparent in the ministry of the Russian *startsy.*

Thus, from the first centuries of the Christian era we may detect a distinction between the spiritual paternity of the *theophori* on one hand, and of the priests and bishops on the other. Although they were equally charismatic, the first was considered as a personal gift, independent of any hierarchic function, whereas the second was linked not to the person but to the pastoral and sacerdotal functions of the Church. Far from being opposites, these two forms of "paternity" were complementary. They had the same aim and effected the same filiation according to two different manners—sacramental or personal. They could be found happily combined in the same person. But nonetheless, their duality witnessed to a fruitful tension between the two poles of the ecclesial life: the harmony of the Son and that of the Spirit, each distinct from the other, and yet conjoined. The sacramental and institutional aspect of the Church is evidence of the objectivity of the grace offered in Christ; its pneumatological

[4] P. Evdokimov, "La paternite spirituelle," in *Contacts* 58 (1967), p. 102.

[5] Simeon the New Theologian, "Treatise on Confession," in K. Holl, *Enthusiasmus und Büssgewalt im griech. Mönchtum* (Leipzig, 1898).

dimension unveils the mystery of the Spirit—its subjective work, to some extent, in the persons with whom it identifies itself. The first aspect is best expressed by the image of the body of Christ. On the other hand, St. Paul saw the Church in a pneumatological perspective when he spoke of it as an edifice which "adjusted herself and grew" by integrating a multitude of persons, each of whom had been called upon to become "a dwelling place of God, in the Spirit".[6]

Such were the doctrinal and historical soil and the spiritual earth in which Orthodox Syrio-Palestinian, Egyptian, Greek and Russian monachism took deep roots. In the tradition of the great charismatic schools, it never ceased to draw nourishment from the sap of a living prophetism in spite of archaisms and even the sclerosis of certain outward forms. We cannot understand the evangelical vigor of the Russian *startsy* of modern times if we ignore the source to which they deliberately came to draw inspiration, not to separate themselves from the institution but to renovate and purify it.

The Image of the "Starets" in Ancient Russian Hagiography

In ancient Russia, lives of saints (*gitie*) constituted a highly appreciated literary genre which, like iconography, obeyed its own rules. Although they did express a spiritual vision, such lives were rather poor in biographical material, strictly speaking, although careful study may help us to discern the personal, prophetic traits of various saints behind the golden haze of legend that envelops them. But, above all, the lives reveal a vision of Christian perfection peculiar to Russia. We may see in them the first outlines of the figure of the "holy Russian monk" —the *starets*.

All we can do here is to make a concise resume of the results of an investigation, already conducted elsewhere, from a mainly phenomenological and historical point of view.[7]

6 Eph. 2, 21-22; cf. V. Lossky, *op. cit.*, p. 171.

7 E. Behr-Sigel, *op. cit.;* for the historical aspect of the problem, see especially G. Fedotov, *Sviatye drevnei Roussi* (The Saints of Ancient Russia) (Paris, 1931).

The most popular "saints' lives" in which whole generations were able to contemplate the ideal image of the holy monk were undoubtedly those of St. Theodosius of Pechera in the Varyag, pre-Mongolian Russia of Kiev, and of St. Sergius of Radonesh in Muscovite Russia. Although they were influenced by Byzantine and—no doubt—Palestinian models, they still retained some original features characteristic of ancient Russian monachism.

Together with St. Antony of Pechera, Theodosius (died 1074) was the founder of the famous Lavra monastery of the Caverns of Kiev. He was also the real organizer of an autocthonous monachism whose evangelical radiance spread throughout Varyag Russia. After bringing the monks out of the "dark and sad" underground caverns in which Antony's first companions had buried themselves, "Father Theodosius" gave the community a Basilian, cenobitic "rule" inspired by that of Studion. It demanded obedience and poverty, and it organized with a certain elasticity the personal spiritual life of the "brothers" within the framework of liturgical, communal prayer.

But above all, the personality of Theodosius impressed the mark of the Spirit, which had inspired him, on the minds of the community. The gentleness of the *starets,* his almost maternal tenderness, his aspiration to follow the humiliated Son of Man literally by accomplishing the humblest tasks and by exposing himself to mockery because of his "wretched clothes"—all shed the light of the beatitudes over this first Russian monachism.

These "poor men" and "gentle men" did, however, play an important part in the social and political as well as the religious life of their people. Thanks to their spiritual labors, a Christianity that had been imported from abroad, and which had been more or less imposed by the ruling classes, did at last really begin to take root in their hearts. People came from all over Varyag Russia to the Monastery of the Caverns to ask for aid and advice, to beg for a blessing or to seal a reconciliation by kissing the cross of the venerable *starets.* Constantly wearing the same "wretched clothes", Theodosius agreed to sit at the Table of the Princes. But he also dared to raise his voice to reproach them for their fratricidal fights or to appeal to their justice to defend the rights of the weak. He is remembered by the Christian Church as one who brought not only a community, but a whole people, to the Christian life by the mere force of the Spirit and humble love.

The same desire to harmonize the contemplative aims of monachism and the demands of human solidarity reappeared three centuries later in the more robust if more mysterious figure of Sergius of Radonesh (1314-1392).[8] He was the initiator of the *poustynniki* (hermit-monk) movement which renewed the exploits of the Egyptian anchorites in the harsh conditions of the Nordic climate and the still virgin forests of central Russia. Sergius devoted himself for several years to solitary prayer in a forest hermitage. He was woodcutter and carpenter by turns, cleared the forest, and with his own hands built the cabin that served him as shelter and oratory. The wild animals that he fed in the winter become the friends of this recluse whose life ex-haled "the scent of fresh pine chips", as one of his modern biog-raphers has written. But Sergius did not repel companions who asked to join him. As a consequence, he ended by finding himself at the head of a community whose life he had to try to regulate despite himself. A veritable monastery was built and became the famous St. Sergius Lavra of the Trinity (now at Zagorsk), the spiritual center of Muscovite Russia.

Wishing to preserve the monks' state of poverty which was the guarantee of their inner freedom, Sergius refused all donations. Similarly he firmly refused the offer to succeed the Metropolitan Alexis of Moscow in his episcopal capacity. But this same spir-itual man was capable of engaging in temporal activities when the salvation of the "people" seemed to require it. A contem-porary of the Muscovite princes, the "gatherers-together of the Russian soil", he supported their centralizing policies (even though his native town of Rostov and his own family had suffered from them), for he judged them to be favorable to peace and union. Like the Orthodox Church as a whole, he was op-posed to any idea of a crusade but he encouraged Dimitri, the

[8] P. Kovalevsky, *Saint Serge de Radonège* (Paris, 1958).

prince of Moscow, to lead his little army against the infinitely more numerous army of the Mongol invaders: "Your duty demands that you defend your people. Be prepared to offer your soul and to shed your blood." [9]

This balance between contemplation and action, between retreat from the age and presence in the world, toward which the spiritual paths of ancient Russia had been leading, was unfortunately upset in the following century. At the beginning of the 16th century, the conflict over the question of monastic *latifundia* which had opposed two holy monks, Nilus Sorski and Joseph of Volok, seemed to consummate the break between two spiritual tendencies which Theodosius and Sergius had been able to synthesize: on one hand, an essentially contemplative and mystical, if somewhat anarchizing, movement represented by the *startsy* of the regions beyond the Volga, with Nilus as its spokesman; on the other hand, a cenobitic monachism, conscious of its social duties, but which was to see the triumph of Joseph's ritualistic legalism. A defender of monastic property, Joseph finally won the day despite the hostility of the prince. By depriving the Russian Church of the free prophetism of the *startsy* who were persecuted by the hierarchy and driven back into their remote hermitages in the north, the victory of the Josephites prepared the schism of the Old Believers.[10]

After being inwardly broken for all its apparent prosperity and deprived of a part of its spiritual substance, Russian monachism was called upon to face the wave of secularization that spread across Russia under Peter the Great in the early 18th century.

The Age of Reason was a dark age for the Russian Church which was being transformed into a simple State mechanism by the abolition of the patriarchate and by the Clerical Regulations of 1721. Catherine II continued Peter's policies by confiscating ecclesiastical lands and by tending to limit recruitment for the

[9] *Idem*, pp. 110ff.
[10] E. Behr-Sigel, *op. cit.*, pp. 76-91; J. Meyendorff, *Une controverse sur le rôle social de l'Eglise* (Chevetogne, 1956).

monasteries as much as possible. All too often the monasteries became mere refuges for nobles escaping from military service or secret strongholds for the Old Beliefs. A new episcopate which had risen out of the "reformed" ecclesiastical schools, and which was subjected to the State bureaucracy, seemed ready to break the last links that bound it to traditional monachism. But even in the darkest days of this spiritual winter there appeared the first signs of that renewal of which the *startsy* movement was a major if not unique aspect.

The "Startsy" Movement

The beginning of the monastic renewal in 19th-century Russia was marked by the revolt of an angry young man, Peter Velitch-kovski (1722-1794), the future *starets* Paissios.[11] A foundation scholar at the ecclesiastical Academy of Kiev where both organization and teaching were modeled on those of Jesuit colleges in nearby Poland, the young seminarian rejected the Latinizing, humanistic—what he himself called "pagan"—teaching that it offered him. It was not so much intellectual activity as such that he was rejecting—he was a brilliant pupil—but a culture modeled on the humanistic, Western type which separated intelligence from the heart—a heart still completely if obscurely impregnated with the mystic experience of the fathers. Peter also extended his reproaches to academic monachism which he considered to be worldly, swollen with vanity and dangerous for the salvation of the soul.

After entering into open conflict with his superiors, the young seminarian abandoned his studies and spent several years as a semi-pilgrim, semi-vagabond, wandering from monastery to monastery along the uncertain frontiers of the Ukraine, and in Moldavia and Poland. He ended by settling in a little Moldavian monastery where he accomplished his first monastic vows at the age of 19. But still in search of a *"starets* after his own heart" and afraid that he might be obliged to receive his sacerdotal

---

[11] S. Tchetverikov, *Moldavskii starets Piassii Velitchkovskii* (Petseri, 1938).

ordination, he fled once more and came to Mount Athos in the summer of 1746. But even there his disappointment was great, since the monastery on the holy mountain was in a state of complete decadence. No one seemed to take an interest in his fate, and it was there that Paissios was to spend the most desolate years of his life in extreme poverty and an almost total spiritual solitude. But it was also at Mount Athos that he made the discovery that changed his entire life. He was constantly seeking for the teachings of the fathers, and by ransacking the libraries of the Serbian and Bulgarian monasteries near his hermitage, he found a hidden treasure: the manuscripts of Nilus Sorski and other Slavic translations of works of hesychast inspiration. The secret he discovered was none other than the "prayer of Jesus", or spiritual prayer, of which Paissios was to make himself the apostle for the rest of his life.

To analyze the nature and significance of this mystic orison which defines hesychast spirituality but has numerous variants is beyond the scope of this study.[12] Let us simply remember that the exterior form taken by the "spiritual prayer" is a repeated, uninterrupted invocation of the name of Jesus, usually combined with certain respiratory rhythms. Its aim, according to hesychastic terminology, is the "descent of the intelligence" into the "inner abysses of the heart", or, in other words, union with Christ by attaining awareness of the dwelling of the Spirit in the depths of the personality which it reestablishes in its integrity.

Filled with enthusiasm by his discovery, Paissios at once wished to share it. He welcomed first one, then several companions. Having at last received his sacerdotal ordination (although not without hesitations) he became the *higoumene* of a community which soon left Athos to settle in Roumania, a country then more favorable to contemplative monachism than Russia. It was there that Paissios died in 1794 at the monastery of Niamets.

Paissios' influence was considerable. He trained numerous monks who swarmed throughout various Orthodox countries,

[12] Cf. Un moine de l'Eglise l'Orient; *La prière de Jesus* (Chevetogne, 1963); E. Behr-Sigel, "La prière de Jesus ou le mystère de la spiritualité monastique orthodoxe," in *Dieu vivant* 8 (1947), pp. 69ff.

expecially in Roumania and Russia. His literary work and his vast correspondence also helped to diffuse his message.

In Roumania, Paissios was the organizer of several communities. He instinctively rediscovered the spiritual equilibrium that was so characteristic of Russian monachism in its beginnings, and he strove to harmonize the retreat necessary to mystical contemplation with the demands of a cenobitic life centered on liturgy—not forgetting the service of his fellow men. It was thus, while preserving the mystical aim of the monk's life, that Paissios admitted the usefulness, even the necessity, of both manual and intellectual work. His communities included several teams of "workers". Some worked in the fields; others devoted themselves to more intellectual tasks such as the translation and printing of patristic works. In winter, the whole community came together for a period of retreat, sustained by prayer, colloquies and spiritual conversations.

Having suffered as a young man from his spiritual abandonment, Paissios tried to organize "spiritual paternity", although without depriving it of its charismatic spontaneity. Like his hesychastic fathers he regarded obedience to the "rule" or to the "spiritual father" as only an apprenticeship or a preliminary stage which, by making the spirit available for grace, led it to union with God and to the glorious freedom of the Son of God.

Paissios himself gave the example of a laborious existence and overflowing charity. He was the author of "chapters" on spiritual prayer [13] as well as of numerous translations of Greek spiritual works into ecclesiastical Slavonic. Of these works, particular mention should be made of his translation of the famous *Philocalia*. It was distributed in Russia under the title *Dobrotolioubvie* (Love of Good) and was extremely popular, even among the common people, as evidenced by the famous *Tales of a Russian Pilgrim*.[14]

Although he became a sick man, Paissios continued to work

[13] Cf. *Besedi o Molitve Iissousovoi* (Remarks on the Prayer of Jesus) (Valaam-Serdopol, 1938), pp. 270ff.
[14] *Récits d'un Pélerin Russe* (Neuchatel, 1943).

sitting by his bed which was covered with books and manuscripts. But he was far from shutting himself up in an ivory
tower, for he opened wide the doors of his monastery to all the
poor, the aged and the sick who had fled from the Russo-Turkish
war of 1768 and who came swarming in, even invading the cells
of the monks.

Paissios' teachings were spread by his disciples in most of the
Orthodox countries. Monks who had been trained either directly
or indirectly by the Moldavian *starets* played an important part
in the monastic renewal in 19th-century Russia. He also made
his influence felt by means of a vast and steady correspondence,
not only with his spiritual children but with such influential members of the hierarchy as the famous metropolitan of St. Petersburg, Gabriel Petrov. A court prelate in great favor with Catherine II (she dedicated her translation of Marmontel's *Belisarius*
to him) who was also in close contact with St. Tychon of Zadonsk, Gabriel always remained a true monk at heart. As a consequence he used his influence in a Russia that was in process of
secularization to restore that mystic tradition of the fathers which
had been rediscovered by Paissios. It was thus that the seeds of a
spiritual springtime that was to blossom in the following century
were implanted in the Russian soil after being brought to it in so
many different ways.

The Optino "Startsy" [15]

Toward the end of the 18th century, the monastery of Optino
(in the government region of Kaluga) had fallen into a state of
complete decline, like many other Russian convents. The community was comprised only of a few aged monks and was men-
aced by physical as well as spiritual extinction. But after being
charmed by the beauty of the site, the metropolitan Platon, the
organizer of theological teaching in Russia, tried to restore monastic life at Optino thereby bringing in some of Paissios' disciples. His effort was continued by the bishop of Kaluga, the future

[15] Cf. I. Smolitsch, *Leben und Lehre der Starzen* (Vienna, 1936);
S. Tchetverikof, *Optino Poustyn* (Paris, 1926); I. Kologrivof, *Essai sur
la Sainteté en Russie* (Bruges, 1952), pp. 398ff.

metropolitan of Kiev, Philaret Amphiteatrov, who built a *skite* not far from the main monastery, for monks who wished to devote themselves to contemplative prayer. This was the hermitage that Dostoevski described in *The Brothers Karamazov*.

In 1829, a former companion of Paissios, Father Leonidus (1768-1841), came to Optino where he inaugurated the line of the great *startsy* which was to continue unbroken until the eve of the 1917 revolution.

Before coming to Optino, Leonidus had already been in spiritual contact with the *starets* Macarius (1788-1860) who succeeded him after first being his closest collaborator.

Macarius had been born in a family which belonged to the cultivated nobility, and he had received careful instruction. But although his education had been superior to that of Leonidus, he considered the latter as his "spiritual father" and even when he was rector of the *skite* at Optino he was unwilling to undertake anything without the latter's advice. For several years, Leonidus and Macarius directed the life of the monks together while also attending to the spiritual needs of the growing numbers of pilgrims who came in thousands to the monastery to consult the *startsy*, to explain their difficulties and to ask for advice, consolation and blessing.

In 1839, a novice, Alexander Grenkov, the future *starets* Ambrosius (1812-1891) entered the monastery. He became the "spiritual son" of the *starets* Leonidus, and when the latter was on the point of death he handed him over "from hand to hand" to the *starets* Macarius, whose collaborator and eventual successor he became. It was under his *startchestvo* that the spiritual influence of Optino was at its most widespread.

Although they were very closely linked spiritually by a veritable transmission of charisma, all three monks were strong personalities with very different characteristics, and the ministry of each was distinguished by its own style.

A man of the people with little scholastic education, a blunt but jovial manner of speech, and an imposing physical presence, Leonidus particularly attracted simple people, whether they were monks or laymen. He had the gift of being able to decipher souls, to understand their hidden language, and to divine their secret thoughts. A man close to humble people, he knew how to find the gesture that would most comfort them and the word that would most console them. The approaches to his cell were often crowded with people, and the *starets* would go from one person to another, blessing pilgrims, reciting prayers over the sick and anoiting them with oil from the little lamp which burned before the ikon of the mother of God. But his activities did not escape criticism. A part of the instructed clergy were scandalized by the "superstitious" practices of the *moujik* in a cassock. Even the bishops, with the exception of the more enlightened like the two philarets of Moscow and Kiev, were mistrustful as they watched the development of this current popular piety that they were ill-equipped to control. Their hostility to the inner freedom of the *startsy* was made manifest by all sorts of restrictions and prohibitions imposed on their activities. As a general rule, the *startsy* submitted, sometimes with a display of sharp temper which belied their monastic gravity. Once when Leonidus had been threatened for receiving and anoiting the sick despite the bishop's prohibition, he cried out: "Let them do with me what they will! They may send me to Siberia, but I shall remain what I am! Look at these sick. Can I refuse them the prayer they are asking for? They put all their hopes in it and, by their faith, it brings them the desired healing."

Leonidus' counsels were distinguished by their practical, intuitive wisdom. Under the *starets* Macarius, a more educated, literate man, the *startchestvo* of Optino entered into a new phase. It became open to problems of thought, culture and the social and political life of Russia, and its influence began to reach a cultivated elite. Thanks to the Kireievski family whose domains were in the neighborhood of Optino and whose friend he became, the *starets* Macarius entered into relations with the circle of Slavophiles. The friendship of the *startsy* orientated the thought of Ivan Kireievski toward patristic theology, from which he extracted the idea of "integral knowledge" as the foundation of a Christian philosophy.[16] These relationships proved equally favorable to the work of translation and publication of the Church Fathers which was undertaken at Optino and in which Kireievski took an active part, successfully arousing the interest of the metropolitan Philaret of Moscow. It was thus that it became possible to publish the "Rule" of Nilus Sorski, the works of Isaac the Syrian, Simeon the New Theologian, Maximus the Confessor and others.

Numerous representatives of the intelligentsia and the enlightened nobility came in pilgrimage to Optino at this time. In 1850 when he was struggling alone, ill and misunderstood even by his friends, Gogol wrote a letter to the Optino *startsy*, imploring them to pray for him and his work. On several occasions he gathered new strength from the monastic peace of the hermitage where the monks—in particular, the *starets* Macarius—appeared to him to be "gay, indulgent, peaceable, affable, having gone beyond the stage of severity". Although Macarius did not succeed in appeasing once and for all the troubled genius of the author of *Dead Souls,* he did aid others like Ivan Kireievski (who became his "spiritual son") to find a way toward faith and the Church and away from the troubled religiosity of German Romanticism. "Under Macarius' direction," wrote V. Lossky,[17] "[Kireievski] succeeded in his philosophical work in bringing about this harmony between exterior obedience and great inner freedom which characterizes the Orthodox thinking." Ivan Kireievski died in 1856 and was buried in the monastery church near the tombs of the *startsy.*

The *starets* Macarius was very fragile in health and led a laborious and austere life, although without any ascetic excess. He ate everything in small quantities, prayed for several hours each day, wrote, and received visitors until late at night. But he generally kept one hour free for himself when he would walk alone in the monastery garden, stopping from time to time to admire a flower at length.

Macarius' meditative spirit, which was spontaneously directed

[16] A. Gratieux, *Khomiakov et le mouvement slavophile* I (Paris, 1939), pp. 72ff.

[17] V. Lossky, "Le starets Macaire," in *Contacts* 37 (1962), pp. 17ff.

toward the problems of inner life, was in violent contrast with the fiery, active spirit and all-embracing curiosity of the *starets* Ambrosius. Bursting with vitality (despite an early infirmity) and with an exceptionally open mind, Ambrosius was as much at his ease in erudite work as in the fields. First and foremost, he was passionately interested in mankind, in men's outer activities as much as in the secret life of their souls which he would read with a strange perspicacity that often bordered on divination. But he was also able to bring all his lucid intelligence to bear on the solution of practical and even technical problems such as the irrigation of arid land. Every human care, be it ever so humble, seemed to him to deserve respect and sympathy. In consequence, when he was dealing with the most varied problems, whether they were those of an old peasant woman trying to raise poultry, the question of religious vocation, or the drama of an unmarried mother expelled from home by her parents, he always showed the same degree of attention and the same desire to find a solution to a situation, be it painful or merely confused. Although he had been a legal zealot in his youth, he later allowed his heart to be submerged by an immense wave of divine compassion. Toward the end of his life, he was often heard to say, as he nodded his head: "I was strict at the beginning of my *startchestvo,* but now I've become weak: people have so much suffering—so much suffering!" [18] He was also quoted as saying: "I would like to bring to each man the blessed joy of God and to help everyone, no matter what the conditions of his life."

Ambrosius annihilated his own subjectivity with an act of total self-offering, and he inwardly identified himself with all who confided in him. "All my life," he said, "all I have ever done has been to cover the roofs of others while my own roof has remained full of holes."

The *starets* Ambrosius' correspondence was enormous. Dozens of letters came to him every day, and they would be laid out on the ground before him while he would point with a stick at those which required an immediate answer.

Although Ambrosius took care to avoid acquiring a reputa-

---

[18] *Idem,* "Le starets Ambroise," in *Contacts* 40 (1962), p. 224.

tion as a thaumaturgist, rumors spread of certain miraculous events and helped to bring crowds to Optino as well as to Chamordino, a convent where the cloistered nuns were his "spiritual daughters" and where he liked to stay. But even such simple souls in search of signs and miracles were joined by cultivated men with sharpened critical faculties, by unbelievers, and by those "seekers after God" who were so numerous among the Russian intelligentsia at the end of the 19th century.

The writer Leontiev, a whimsical, passionate man, came to seek peace at Optino where he stayed for several years until he finally became a monk on the advice of Father Ambrosius, at the monastery of the Saint Sergius Trinity in 1890.

V. Rozanov and Vladimir Soloviev also came as pilgrims. Soloviev came with Dostoevski who had lost little Aliosha, the youngest of his children, only a few months previously. As his wife wrote: "F. M. met the famous Father Ambrosius three times: once in the midst of the crowd and twice in private." We do not know what was the secret of these interviews. But Anna Grigorievna thought that the *starets* had told her husband those same words of consolation that the writer put in the mouth of his character, the *starets* Zosima: ". . . and do not take comfort, for you must not take comfort. . . . Do not take comfort but weep. And for a long time to come you will shed these great maternal tears, but in the end they will transform themselves into tears of sweet joy and your bitter tears will be no more than tears of that sweet tenderness and inner purification which save from sin. As for your little child, I will mention it in my prayers. What was his name?" "Alexis, Father." [19] Dostoevski left the hermitage of Optino somewhat more peaceful in mind, and then began to write his great novel *The Brothers Karamazov*.

Leo Tolstoy also knew Fr. Ambrosius and came one day to talk with him. When, at the end of his life, the excommunicated prophet fled from his family home to attempt a final reconciliation between his life and his ideals, he wandered for several days

[19] C. Motchoulsky, *Dostoïevski, l'Homme et l'Oeuvre* (Paris, 1963), p. 482.

around Optino and Chamordino (where one of his sisters had retired) before going to Astapovo to die.

Thus it was that, as V. Lossky wrote, "all the spiritual paths in late 19th-century Russia converged at Optino".[20]

Now that we have come to the end of this survey, let us try to answer the question: In what did the novelty of the 19th century-Russian *startsy* consist? And to what extent may we speak of "prophetism" with regard to the *startsy?*

One thing is certain: they did not consider themselves to be innovators. On the contrary, we will find that the beginning of the movement was characterized by a wish to renew the authentic spiritual tradition of the Church—that of "the fathers who were filled with God and whose divine deeds shone forth like the sun . . . throughout the Orient, and later at Constantinople, on the holy Mount Athos, in many islands and recently also, by the grace of God, in Greater Russia".[21]

But this return to the source was also a return to the essential source—that of the Father of light whose paternity of love had never ceased to inspire the charismatic ministry of the *startsy.* For the *startsy,* the reading of the spiritual works of the fathers was not a pretext for an endless repetition of past formulas but an initiation to a spiritual path in which their creative fidelity could be made manifest.

One of the characteristic traits of the *startsy* was that they always showed great discretion with regard to the intimate details of their spiritual life. But we do know that the hidden source from which it drew its strength and light was prayer, and, more particularly, that known as the "prayer of Jesus". Paissios' rediscovery of the spirit and methods of hesychasm was a spiritual event of considerable importance for Russian Orthodoxy after the current of the great mystical wave had been swallowed up, in the 17th and 18th centuries, by the sands of formal, ritualistic piety. Now, thanks to the *startsy,* the "prayer of Jesus" was once

[20] V. Lossky, *ibid.,* p. 230.
[21] "Lettre de Paissios aux ennemis et calomniateurs de la Priere de Jesus," in Un moine de l'Eglise d'Orient, *op. cit.,* pp. 63ff.

again uttered in tune with the beating of the human heart, not only in the silence of monasteries and hermitages but amid the noise and bustle of towns and villages.

The special characteristic of Russian hesychasm, especially that which shone forth from Optino, was its great spiritual warmth in a climate of sobriety and evangelical simplicity. Lightened by the conceptual apparatus of a palamism,[22] which was originally destined to protect the mystical orison of the solitaries (but which had ended by imprisoning it), hesychasm now regained its original fervor and aims: a summons to a real encounter with the living God in the prayer of the name of Jesus. It affirmed that this encounter was not darkness but light which, by illuminating the heart, also illuminated the world: "Through the heart, the light of the name of Jesus illumines all the universe." [23] Taken in this sense and sustained by a breathing technique which was not essential but which did aid spiritual concentration, the "prayer of Jesus" could accompany every activity. Both simple illiterates and men of learning could practice it. It was an expression of the royal priesthood of all believers; it sanctified every human deed and became "an instrument for the secret offering of each thing and each person, a setting of the divine seal upon the world".[24]

No doubt, the *startsy* did not express all these ideas textually. But they did make them germinate in the hearts of those—religious or secular—whom they initiated into prayer or simply advised with kindness as they followed their different paths in the world.

The new and prophetic factor—at least, in its breadth and depth if not in its principle—was the universal ministry of the *startsy*. In this respect also, no doubt, they were renewing their

[22] Doctrine of Gregory Palamas who formulated the distinction between divine essence and energies in the 14th century, thus providing a theological basis for the mystic exprience of the hesychasts; cf. J. Meyendorff, *Introduction a l'etude de Gregoire Palamas* (Paris, 1959).

[23] S. Boulgakoff, *L'Orthodoxie* (Paris, 1932), p. 207.

[24] N. Gorodetzky, "The Prayer of Jesus," in *Blackfriars* (1942), pp. 74-78.

links with the most ancient tradition of Russian monachism which had been that of Theodosius of Pechera and Sergius of Radonesh. But they were acting in entirely different historical circumstances and the style of their ministry was new in itself. In the early days of Russian Christianity, the "holy monks" were the educators of the people and princes alike, and were called upon to guide, judge and even directly shape their actions. In the profoundly secularized Russia of the 19th century, the work of the *startsy* was essentially an inner one. It no longer aimed at acting directly on the course of events or at transforming social structures but at touching and enlightening men's hearts—i.e., the essence of the human personality in all its mysterious freedom. This did not mean, however, that the *startsy* had lost interest in the world or that, having reached the shore, they were able to contemplate with serenity the beating of the waves against a vessel whose wreck they could foresee. The *starets* Macarius followed the events of the Crimean War with anguish and St. Seraphim of Sarov [25] was "in tears" as he foretold the calamities and sufferings which were to afflict the Russian people.

We may regret that the *startsy* did not raise their voices against the social injustices and ecclesiastical abuses as Tychon of Zadonsk had dared to do in the 18th century. But by opening the doors of their monasteries wide to the multitude, to its needs and cares (thus greatly scandalizing some ecclesiastical authorities), were they not protesting implicitly against the indifference and inattention to temporal realities of which too many men of the Church were guilty?

By his living sympathy for everything concerning man, his problems and his activities, was not a man like Ambrosius silently affirming that no domain of human life should remain alien to the grace of the Christ who could and must save and illuminate all?

[25] Saint Seraphim of Sarov (1759-1833). The limits of this article do not leave space in which to deal more fully with the greatest Russian mystic of the 19th century, since he did not belong directly to the "school" of the *startsy*. Cf. V. Iljine, *Prepodobnyi Seraim Sarovskii* (Paris, 1930).

No one, perhaps, was better able to formulate the implicit doctrine of the *startsy* in theological terms than the brilliant and obscure Bukharev,[26] their contemporary. Above all, the *startsy* had invented a style for the presence of the spiritual in the world which was in accordance with men's needs: a compassionate love which helped man to bear the burden of his solitude and guilt; an intelligent sympathy which attempted to unravel the knot of his problems and neuroses in the light of some supernatural joy. With the persons of Ambrosius of Optino and St. Seraphim of Sarov who welcomed each visitor with the paschal greeting "Christ is risen", the *startsy* were offering all men a spirituality impregnated with paschal and pentecostal joy.

May we go even further and, like several contemporary Orthodox thinkers, discern a call to go beyond the monastic "spiritual paternity", and even beyond the traditional forms or monachism, in the message of the *startsy?* [27]

"You will leave these walls. I bless you in view of a great task to be accomplished in the world." The words spoken by the *starets* Zosima to Aliosha Karamazov may certainly never have been pronounced in historical reality. Nonetheless, St. Seraphim of Sarov did say to Motovilov:

"As to the fact that you are a layman and I a monk, there is no need to dwell on that. . . . The Lord is seeking for hearts that are filled with love for him and for his fellow men. This is the throne on which he likes to be seated and on which he appears in the plenitude of his celestial glory. For it is in the heart of man that the kingdom of God resides. . . . The Lord hears the prayer of the monk and the simple layman equally well, for even if their faith is only a 'mustard seed' it may still move mountains." [28]

[26] A. M. Bukharev (Archimandrite Theodore) (1824-1871), a Russian theologian, monk, priest and professor of theology who had himself reduced to lay status without leaving the Orthodox Church. His main work was *L'Orthodoxie et le Monde Contemporain*, (St. Petersburg, 1860); cf. B. Zenkowsky, *Histoire de la Philosophie Russe* I (Paris, 1952), pp. 350ff.

[27] P. Evdokimov, *op. cit.,* p. 104.

[28] Saint Seraphim of Sarov, "Entretien avec Motovilov," in *Le Semeur* (March-April, 1927).

This, perhaps, is the final message of the Russian *startsy*. By rising out of the heart of their Church, by taking nourishment from its sacramental and spiritual sap, they liberated the ever-flowing source of immortal life from the dross accumulated by the historical sins of Christendom, for the sake of all mankind, their brethren.

Charles Dessain, Cong. Orat./*Birmingham, England*

Cardinal Newman
as Prophet

E ven when he was at Oxford Newman was regarded as a prophet.
One person (not a High Church-
man), who had come under his influence, later testified: "A mysterious veneration had by degrees gathered round him, till now it
was almost as though some Ambrose or Augustine of elder ages
had reappeared." His power showed itself when he spoke of
"Unreal Words", "The Individuality of the Soul", "The Invisible
World", "Particular Providence", "The Ventures of Faith",
"Warfare, the Condition of Victory" or "The Cross of Christ, the
Measure of the World." The very titles of these sermons suggest
the prophet's message. After World War I the German New-
manist, Eric Przywara, called Newman "the peculiar and unique
Augustinus redivivus of modern times, and that because his gaze
is calmly fixed upon the God of the end". And now it has become
commonplace to speak of Newman as a prophet in connection
with Vatican Council II.[1]

Yet if Newman is to be thought of as a prophet, he was also

[1] J. C. Shairp, *Studies in Poetry and Philosophy* (1886), pp. 244 and
248; Eric Przywara, "St. Augustine and the Modern World," in *A
Monument to Saint Augustine* (London, 1930); B. C. Butler, "Newman
and the Second Vatican Council," in *The Rediscovery of Newman: An
Oxford Symposium*, edited by John Coulson and A. M. Allchin (London,
1967), p. 235. See also Giovanni Velocci, *Newman al Concilio* (Rome,
1966).

very much a man, and not only a man, but a humanist. He realized vividly the unseen world, but was intensely interested in the persons and the world around him and all that related to them. From his schooldays until ripe old age he was full of activity and surrounded by friends. His earliest Oxford University sermon was entitled "The Philosophical Temper First Enjoined by the Gospel", and he described the purpose of the Catholic University he founded as the "enlargement of mind" of those who attended it. On becoming a Catholic he adopted the institute of the humanist St. Philip, where no vows are taken, and his friends joined him in it. He made quite clear that he infinitely preferred a gentle reforming prophet like St. Philip to one such as Savonarola. What struck all who knew Newman was the absence of pomposity, that naturalness which is the consequence of sincerity with oneself. He revealed himself when he made his pagan heroine, Callista, remark that "there was a higher beauty than that which the order and harmony of the natural world revealed, and a deeper peace and calm then that which the exercise, whether of the intellect or the purest human affection, can supply". She came to understand that Christians "were detached from the world, not because they had not the possession, nor the natural love of its gifts, but because they possessed a higher blessing already, which they loved above everything else".[2]

There is one further characteristic of Newman's work as a religious leader or prophet that must be made clear before we can discuss it in detail, and that is its unity. From his first conversion at sixteen, when he gave a real assent with mind and heart to the Christian faith—or, more precisely, from his Anglican ordination in 1824—he had one single purpose: the promotion and defense of the revealed religion of Christianity. This purpose dated from long before the Oxford Movement, and after his conversion to the Catholic Church it continued unchanged. Thus he was never one of those prophets who, in their preoccupation with their mission, lack the shepherd's solicitude for his flock. All of Newman's activities—literary and educational as well as the

[2] John Henry Newman, *Callista* (uniform edition), p. 327.

more strictly religious ones—had a pastoral aim. He always wrote from within the Christian community, and his lectures, pamphlets, sermons and other works had an immediate apostolic purpose. He covered many fields; he did not compose scientific treatises, but he was not a dilettante. His passionate devotion to the cause of revealed religion was the secret of his style. He wrote, as he preached, for definite people, and he was not, in a technical sense, a theologian. Rather, his whole personality was engaged, and what he proclaimed and defended was a personal and living theology.

In fact, an overriding purpose is by no means the only factor that gives his work its unity. Although he did not write scientific treatises, a thoroughly coherent unified system underlay his thinking. He rejected all the abstract, all the rationalist philosophies, and insisted that truth was grasped by the personal reasoning of each individual. The concrete was primary. Certainty resided in the mind, not in propositions outside it. His philosophy was based on the psychology of the individual, on the personal assents he made, not on conceptual thought, inferences or syllogisms. He considered the human mind as it actually worked, and this psychological, phenomenological approach was also a metaphysical one, because of his belief in a divine providence that had so arranged things. Philosophy was the personal testimony of living persons, not impersonal reasoning. In metaphysics and ethics, as well as in religious inquiry, "egotism is true modesty", and "each of us can speak only for himself; he cannot lay down the law; he can only bring his own experiences to the common stock of psychological facts." Thus true modesty did not consist in claiming scientific approval for conclusions, but in stating what were personally one's own grounds for holding them. Finally, Newman's views changed surprisingly little. The fundamental principles underlying the work of his maturity can be found in embryo in his earliest writings.[3]

[3] *An Essay in Aid of a Grammar of Assent* (uniform edition), pp. 384-86; A. J. Boekraad, *The Personal Conquest of Truth according to John Henry Newman* (Louvain, 1955); M. Nedoncelle, *La philosophie religieuse de John Henry Newman* (Strasbourg, 1946); *The Philosophi-*

Religion concerned with Persons

In view of what has been said, it is not surprising that the first religious truth which Newman made his own, and then impressed on others, was, quite simply, that for the Christian, religion is a personal relationship between himself and his creator. Before his first conversion, when toying with the rationalism of the 18th century, Newman wanted to be virtuous, not religious, nor did he understand the meaning of loving God. After his conversion he had a vivid sense of the presence of God, of his Savior's loving particular providential care of each individual, and of the personal gift of the Holy Spirit. In his first book, he described the great benefit of revelation: "It clears up all doubt about the existence of God as separate from and independent of nature, and shows that the world depends not merely on a system, but on a being, real, living and individual." The same book treats of the doctrine of the Blessed Trinity, and explains how simple men have a practical devotion to Father, Son and Holy Spirit, no less acceptable "because it does not happen to be conceived in those precise statements which presuppose the action of the mind on its own sentiments and notions". As time goes on the inward vision will be analyzed and "thus the systematic doctrine of the Trinity may be considered as the shadow, projected for the contemplation of the intellect, of the object of scripturally-informed piety".[4]

Here, as we shall see later, is already the development of doctrine, but for the moment we are concerned to show how Newman makes the Christian life a supremely personal matter. In revelation God offers us his friendship, telling us by deeds and words that he loves us. Again and again Newman emphasizes in his preaching and teaching the Christian privilege of the indwelling in the soul of the Holy Spirit and, through him, of the

---

cal Notebook of John Henry Newman, edited by Edward Sillem, Vol. I, "General Introduction to the Study of Newman's Philosophy" (Louvain, 1968); J. H. Walgrave, O.P., *Newman the Theologian* (London, 1960).

[4] *The Arians of the Fourth Century* (uniform edition), pp. 184 and 143-45.

Father and the Son. He rejects the inadequate ideas of justification held by Protestants or by Catholics in his day. The former
laid stress rather on believing than on the object of belief; the
latter thought of grace as a quality in the soul. Both tended to fix
the mind on self rather than, as the Gospel required, on an indwelling God in whom "we live and move and have our being".
For Newman, however, *"this* is to be justified, to receive the
divine presence within us, and to be made a temple of the Holy
Ghost". Grace was not a mere quality in the soul, but a personal
favor, a loving presence. Newman refused to separate the presence of God as a friend from the change in his creature that was
a consequence of that presence.[5]

Newman's personalism, which showed itself in his many
friendships, is nowhere more clearly seen than in his way of
speaking about our Lord. Those who have not accepted revealed
religion are haunted with the doubt that in following their
noblest instincts and aspirations they may be following an empty
shadow, whereas revelation puts before us Jesus, the risen Christ.
"The life of Christ brings together and concentrates truths concerning the chief good and laws of our being, which wander idle
and forlorn over the surface of the moral world. . . . The philos-
opher aspires toward a divine principle, the Christian toward a
divine agent." [6]

Dedication to the service of this person is the occasion of the
highest virtues, and it is the thought of Christ, not a corporate
body or a system of doctrine, that inspires the zeal of his followers. Newman's sermons put what is unseen vividly before us, and
Christ is at the core of all his writing—for instance, the scintillat-

[5] *Lectures on the Doctrine of Justification* (uniform edition), p. 144.
See also C. S. Dessain, "Cardinal Newman and the Doctrine of Un-
created Grace," in *Clergy Review* (April, 1962), pp. 207-25; (May,
1962), pp. 269-88; C. S. Dessain, "The Biblical Basis of Newman's Ecumenical Theology," in *The Rediscovery of Newman: An Oxford Symposium,* pp. 100-122. More than a century beforehand Newman fulfilled
the requirements laid down by Gerard Philips in "De ratione instituendi
tractatum de Gratia nostrae sanctificationis," in *Eph. Theol. Lou.* (April-
Sept. 1953), p. 357.

[6] *Fifteen Sermons Preached before the University of Oxford* (uniform
edition), pp. 27-28.

ing letters to *The Times* of 1841: "Persons influence us, voices melt us, looks subdue us, deeds inflame us. . . . Christianity is a history supernatural and almost scenic: it tells us what its author is by telling us what he has done." [7] Unlike so many of the Christian thinkers in his day and for long after, Newman did not forget that Christ was now risen and glorified. He preached the importance of the resurrection for our salvation a century before the exegetes and theologians had restored to the paschal mystery its rightful emphasis. There are many eloquent passages on this theme in the *Sermons* and in *Lectures on Justification,* which show the connection between Christ's departure from this earth and his return in the person of and with his Spirit. "He dies to purchase what he rose again to apply. . . . He atones in his own person; he justifies through his Spirit." [8]

Although he thus puts before people the supreme privileges of the Christian, Newman was the last person to do so without laying deep foundations. He had a horror of unreality and of "unreal words", and a vivid sense of the holiness of God and of the judgment in store for each individual man. The Christian faith was to be lived, not talked about. His sermons, whether preached or published, roused men from torpor and produced a revival of the spiritual life in England. The first, in his first volume of *Parochial Sermons,* was entitled "Holiness Necessary for Future Blessedness", and it was at once followed by others on "The Immortality of the Soul" and "Self-Denial, the Test of Religious Earnestness". If we are to live a risen life with Christ, we must first die with him. He was preaching to lay people whose duty it was to take their place in the world, and for whom other-worldliness was not the danger. He insisted on hidden detachment, and so effective was his teaching that he had to warn

[7] John Henry Newman, "The Tamworth Reading Room," in *Discussions and Arguments on Various Subjects* (uniform edition), pp. 293 and 296. See also C. S. Dessain, *John Henry Newman* (London, 1966), pp. 22-24.

[8] *Lectures on the Doctrine of Justification,* Lecture IX: "Righteousness: The Fruit of Our Lord's Resurrection." Cf. *The Constitution on the Sacred Liturgy* of Vatican Council II.

against undertaking humble tasks or secret vows of continence before counting the cost.

He did, however, revive in the Church of England this part of the Gospel. From Hurrell Froude, Newman had learned the Catholic teaching on the intrinsic excellence of virginity, and in a sermon on "The Judaism of the Present Day" he drew attention to the low standard of the time: "If there is one grace in which Christianity stands in especial contrast to the old religion, it is that of purity. Christ was born of a virgin; he remained a virgin; his beloved disciple was a virgin; he abolished polygamy and divorce, and he said that there would be those who for the kingdom of heaven's sake would be even as he. . . . But now, my brethren, who will question that the way of the world at present is to deny that there is such a gift. . . . Does not this show that we have fallen back into the Jewish state?"

Newman tried to introduce among Anglicans the Gospel ideal. He wrote of Saints Basil and Gregory: "When once they had resolved to devote themselves to the service of religion, the question arose how they might best improve and employ the talents committed to them. Somehow, the idea of marrying and taking orders, or taking orders and marrying . . . did not suggest itself to their minds. They fancied they must give up wife, children and property if they would be perfect." [9]

History and Revelations

At the time of his first conversion Newman learned to rest in the thought of himself and his creator, and in his *Apologia* he rejoiced that the Catholic Church reinforced this attitude, and allowed no image, no sacrament "not even the Blessed Virgin herself, to come between the soul and its creator. . . . He alone has redeemed; before his awful eyes we go in death; in the vision of him is our eternal beatitude." [10]

Newman's first vision was incomplete, but involved no refusal of the social aspect of Christianity. This is clear from the ease

[9] *Parochial and Plain Sermons* VI (uniform edition), p. 187; *Historical Sketches* II, pp. 55-56; cf. *Essays Critical and Historical* II, pp. 293-

with which he accepted and preached the doctrine of the Church after entering Anglican orders. His grasp of it increased as he pursued the task of *resourcement,* steeping himself in the teaching of Holy Scripture and the Fathers, and trying to regain the Christian truth in its freshness. Here is one more example of a prophetic attitude. The fear soon arose, however, that this might be mere antiquarianism, since it was of the essence of revealed religion to submit to a positive and living system. It was necessary to explain the meaning of belief in "the holy Catholic Church". Newman wrote his *Lectures on the Prophetical Office* to show that the Church of England was "the nearest approximation to that primitive truth which Ignatius and Polycarp enjoyed, and which the nineteenth century has lost".

Eventually, as is well known, he claimed that it was history which led him to reject that parallel, and to recognize in the Church of Rome the communion of St. Ambrose and St. Athanasius. For the Church, though a mysterious reality of grace, was visible. She was the manifestation in history of God's plan of salvation, and was thus a kind of sacrament. Yet this present living Church was not independent of history. In her, revelation was preserved, and although her members grasped it by a kind of instinct with the help of the Holy Spirit, it was an objective teaching. This was shown by the veneration for Holy Scripture, and by the Church's claim that her doctrines in every age were the echo of the age which preceded it, back until apostolic times. Thus the approach to theology must be historical, and the doctrines of Christianity must be discernible in antiquity.

As has been mentioned, in his first book, *The Arians of the Fourth Century,* Newman was brought up against the historical phenomenon that revelation had undergone a certain development, even in the first three Christian centuries. A few years later his controversy with the liberal Dr. Hampden led him to think out still further the relation between revelation and its statement

---

94. See also Meriol Trevor, *Newman, the Pillar of the Cloud* (London, 1962), pp. 88-96.
    [10] *Apologia pro Vita Sua* (uniform edition), p. 195.

in creeds and dogmas. Eventually in 1843, in the last of his university sermons, he dealt with the historical problem *ex professo*. He began by insisting that the knowledge a Christian had by his faith was something real, permanent, personal and distinct from its explicit statement. "The absence, or partial absence, or incompleteness of dogmatic statements is no proof of the absence of impressions or implicit judgments, in the mind of the Church. Even centuries might pass without formal expression of a truth, which had been all along the secret life of millions of faithful souls."

Newman's own words are more convincing than any paraphrase. "Religious men, according to their measure, have an idea or vision of the Blessed Trinity in unity, of the Son incarnate and of his presence, not as a number of qualities, attributes and actions, not as the subject of a number of propositions, but as one and individual, and independent of words, as an impression conveyed through the senses." And again: "As God is one, so the impression which he gives of himself is one; it is not a thing of parts; it is not a system; . . . it is the vision of an object. When we pray, we pray not to an assemblage of notions, or to a creed, but to one individual being; and when we speak of him we speak of a person, not of a law or a manifestation. This being the case, all our attempts to delineate our impressions of him go to bring out one idea, not two or three or four; not a philosophy, but an individual idea in its separate aspects."

Thus the Christians who form the Church are led to make statements concerning the object of their adoration, and what is essentially an impression on the mind and imagination has become a system and a creed. "The developments in the doctrines of the Holy Trinity and the incarnation are mere portions of the original impression, and modes of representing it." It is necessary to put this personal revelation into language in order to teach and transmit it. The Christian mind reasons not as though from a series of logical propositions, but as being divinely enlightened and as possessed by a sacred impression. "Creeds and dogmas live in the one idea which they are designed to express, and which alone is substantive; and they are necessary only because the human mind cannot reflect upon that idea except piecemeal, cannot use it in its oneness and entireness."

This sermon was doubly prophetic. Newman was describing 120 years beforehand what was to be one of the chief insights of Vatican Council II—namely that the truth of revelation is not a mere series of propositions, but "shines forth for us in Christ who is at once the mediator and the fullness of revelation". The sermon also shows Newman's own prophetic grasp of Christian truth, "the vision of an object", the self-disclosure of God which, far from being enclosed in the propositions necessary to state it, would not be exhausted by many more. Hence, the Anglican Newman points out that to want to have every Catholic doctrine in so many words in Scripture is to be the slave of the letter, and he adds: "To object, then, to the number of propositions upon which an anathema is placed is altogether to mistake their use; for their multiplication is not intended to enforce many things but to express one." [11]

Years later, in *A Grammar of Assent,* Newman still had to meet the objection of those who urged that salvation consisted not in believing propositions *that* there is a God, a Savior, a Trinity, which they regarded as something merely formal and human, but in believing *in* God, *in* a Savior, *in* a sanctifier. "They are right," Newman admits, "so far as this, that men can and sometimes do rest in the propositions themselves" which have their necessary uses, but "they are wrong when they maintain that men need to do so or always do so. . . . We must know concerning God before we can feel love, fear, hope, or trust toward him. . . . The formula, which embodies a dogma for the theologian, readily suggests an object for the worshiper".[12]

The doctrine of development Newman propounded in his last university sermon, he put to a practical use in his book on the

---

[11] *Fifteen Sermons preached before the University of Oxford,* pp. 328-36; cf. *Dogmatic Constitution on Divine Revelation* of Vatican Council II, n. 2.

[12] *An Essay in Aid of a Grammar of Assent,* pp. 120-21; cf. *Dogmatic Constitution on Divine Revelation,* nn. 2-8.

subject. It enabled him to remove his last difficulty in identifying the modern Catholic Church with that of the Fathers. The later Catholic doctrines and practices were the result of "a vivid realization of the original *depositum"*. Newman used various parallels to show that such a development was antecedently probable and to be expected. He asserted most definitely, however, that after the event of the incarnation, there could be no addition to the public revelation given to the Church. The initial impression could only be developed by means of propositions that could never exhaust it. No further teacher was to come. It was the last age, and all the developments were in some sense in Scripture. The consistency of the developments provided a further argument. The orderly growth pointed to a divine guidance in the Roman Church.[13]

Conscience and Faith

Newman's prophetic mission can be traced in both his Anglican and his Catholic life, and cannot be divided neatly into compartments. His was always a religion of persons; he returned to the authentic sources for his Christianity; for him revelation in its fullness was Christ himself. These points can be most easily illustrated from his Anglican career. His other major themes— conscience as the voice of God; obedience to it as the way to faith; the Church as a communion, not a mere organization; the place of the laity; the limitations of infallibility; ecumenism —are developed more fully after he has become a Catholic.

Newman always insisted that conscience was "the voice of God". He knew well enough how in modern times, long before psychoanalysis, great efforts were made to dismiss it as a mere work of man. He based his doctrine on the facts as he saw them. "The child keenly understands that there is a difference between right and wrong. . . . His mind reaches forward with a strong presentiment to the thought of a moral governor, sovereign over

[13] See also the article by H. F. Davis, "Doctrine, Development of," in *A Catholic Dictionary of Theology* (London, 1967), pp. 182-87, and Jean Stern, *Bible et Tradition chez Newman, aux originis de theorie du developpement* (Paris, 1967).

him, mindful and just. It comes to him like an impulse of nature to entertain it." He noted that each man had within him a moral dictate, "an authoritative voice, bidding him do certain things and avoid others". Its injunctions were not always clear in particular cases, not always consistent, but it praised, blamed and issued commands. In fact, although indivisible, its action was twofold. It was a dictate or sense of duty. It was also a judgment of the reason that certain acts were good and certain others wicked, which persisted even where the obligation, the duty, was rejected. A man had not the power over it, or only with extreme difficulty, and he could never entirely destroy it.[14]

Thus conscience, from the nature of the case, carries our mind to a being outside ourselves, and far superior to us, with a peremptory claim on our obedience. Not only does it instruct us to a certain extent but it leads us to the idea of an unseen teacher. It is not merely subjective or even exclusively a moral faculty, but transcendent. The more men listen to and obey it, the clearer it becomes until it produces an intimate perception and sense of the one God. God is not reached by abstract external proofs but by a man's whole personality. As he purifies and strengthens this by faithfulness to his true self, he becomes disposed to accept and believe in the true God.

Newman showed how in ordinary matters knowledge depends on personality. The man of the world, thanks to a wide experience, can size up those he meets, almost at a glance, and for him it is a very valuable asset. He could not put into words why he is prepared to trust this man and not that. His sharpened mind is working in its natural concrete manner. Similarly, in the sphere of religion, it is his moral disposition, his mind sharpened by obedience to conscience, which enables a man to realize the unseen and to have faith. It is not arguments that convince him, although these have their place and may enable him to justify his position with others. Moral dispositions are the road to the truth.

Obedience to conscience leads men further still. Often they

[14] *An Essay in Aid of a Grammar of Assent,* pp. 112 and 104.

cannot decide how much the "true inward guide commands, and how much comes from a mere earthly source. So that the gift of conscience raises a desire for what it does not itself fully supply. ... It creates in them a thirst, an impatience, for the knowledge of that unseen Lord, and governor, and judge, who as yet speaks to them only secretly". Hence the conscientious man is led to look out for a revelation. The definition of a religious man who is not a Christian is that he is on the lookout. This, Newman explains, is why faith receives such praise in the Gospel and incredulity such blame. Moral dispositions lead to faith—that is, to an entire submission to God—and thus our great internal teacher of religion is our conscience. It is a personal guide, even though, since men do not live alone, external assistance may be necessary to help it into action.[15]

The last book Newman wrote contains a short treatise on the whole subject, and in it he shows how conscience is the source of natural law. "I say then that the supreme being is of a certain character, which, expressed in human language, we call ethical. He has the attributes of justice, truth, wisdom, sanctity, benevolence, mercy, as eternal characteristics in his nature, the very law of his being, identical with himself; and next, when he became creator, he implanted this law, which is himself, in the intelligence of all his rational creatures. . . . This law, as apprehended in the minds of individual men, is called 'conscience'; and though it may suffer refraction in passing into the intellectual medium of each, it is not therefore so affected as to lose its character of being the divine law, but has still, as such, the prerogative of commanding obedience." [16]

[15] *Sermons Preached on Various Occasions:* "Dispositions for Faith," pp. 64-67. See also the article by J. H. Crehan, "Conscience," in *A Catholic Dictionary of Theology*, pp. 103, 104. It is not possible here to do more than point out how consonant Newman's teaching is with that of Vatican Council II in the *Declaration on Religious Freedom* and in the *Constitution on the Church in the Modern World*, n. 16. For his views on the non-Christian religions, see *An Essay on the Development of Christian Doctrine* (uniform edition), pp. 380-82.

[16] "A Letter to the Duke of Norfolk," in *Difficulties of Anglicans* II, p. 246. See also D. C. Duivestein, "Reflexions on Natural Law," in *Clergy Review* (April, 1967), pp. 283-94.

The natural law then is not something external or abstract. It derives from conscience, the voice of God, and it is paramount. Each man has the duty of obeying it, and therefore the right to be allowed to do so. Newman shows that this does not mean we may think, speak or act as we like without any thought of God at all. Conscience is "a stern monitor", not "the right of self-will". The natural law is distilled from it only when we are faithful to it. If we would discover the natural law, the consciences of good men must be consulted. In the case of those who have submitted to revelation, it will be a first principle that not only the natural but also the revealed law must be obeyed.

The Church as a Communion

If the consciences of individuals enable them to discover the natural law, all the more do the minds of faithful Christians in the Church, enlightened by the Holy Spirit, enable them to understand the teaching of revelation. The teaching is set forth in the creeds, but it is the personal possession of Christian minds, and is passed on from generation to generation.

Newman's personalism and his sense of the Church as a body existing in history led him naturally to regard it in the first place as a communion. The Church was all her members. These were divided into communities, under bishops who "had their thrones in the Church of divine right" and were the successors of the apostles. He also held what we now call the doctrine of the collegiality of bishops. Yet he had no tendency to identify the Church with her hierarchy. She consisted of the whole People of God. He insisted that "the Christian Church is simply and literally a party or society instituted by Christ. He bade us keep together". Fellowship and mutual sympathy were a duty.[17]

At Oxford he had preached a spirituality for laymen; as a Catholic all his enterprises, those he succeeded in and those in which he was frustrated, were intended to serve and benefit

[17] *Sermons Preached on Various Occasions:* "Order, the Witness and Instrument of Unity," pp. 191-97; *Essays Critical and Historical* II, p. 44; *Parochial and Plain Sermons* VII, pp. 241-42.

them. Since the revealed truth was passed down in the living minds of the millions of the faithful who treasured it, all the baptized, including the laity, must be consulted in matters of doctrine, which they might at times preserve more faithfully than the bishops. To discover what was the mind of the Church, it was necessary to find out what all believed.

This subject has been so much studied in recent years that it is not necessary to develop it here, but it provides a very striking example of the prophetic character of Newman's thought.[18] On the other hand, he was not unaware of the dangers to which the faith of the laity was exposed. Their devotion could degenerate into superstition, and here theology must play its appointed role and restore the balance. Newman's ideal was an educated laity who understood their faith.

From these various considerations it followed that freedom of discussion in the Church was most necessary. The Church was a communion, the truth was reached by many individuals working together, and in matters of faith its mind must be left free to make itself known. This question was discussed in the famous Chapter V of the *Apologia,* "Position of My Mind since 1845", but already in various lectures at Dublin, Newman had shown his confidence that truth could never contradict truth, and that freedom of discussion was necessary not only in scientific and historical matters, but also for theology. He protested that the greatest of scandals was to try to hush up scandals in the history of the Church. Yet, as we have seen, he was always a pastor, and he had a strong objection to the saying of "startling"

---

[18] Newman insisted that the laity shares in the Church's infallibility, and he showed how, in the Arian controversy of the 4th century, "the divine tradition committed to the infallible Church was proclaimed and maintained far more by the faithful than by the episcopate": *On Consulting the Faithful in Matters of Doctrine,* edited with an introduction by John Coulson (London, 1961), p. 75. See also C. S. Dessain, *John Henry Newman,* pp. 111-18. A true prophet, Newman was very unpopular with the dominant authorities for insisting on the importance of the laity, but his doctrine has been proclaimed by Vatican Council II, and indeed was one of its leading motifs. See *Dogmatic Constitution on the Church* nn. 12 and 30-31.

things without need, to speaking in an exaggerated or paradoxical way that would upset people, instead of "doing the truth in charity".

This was not to hinder free discussion among the more expert. Although Newman preferred a pluralist society to that of the Middle Ages, he held up the intellectual freedom of the medieval universities as an example. Theories were discussed freely in one university after another and the matter was hammered out. One bishop here or there might intervene and still the controversy raged, and generations would pass before a decision was reached at Rome. Very different was the state of affairs in 1864 when everything was reported to a centralized papacy and signs of approval or disapproval made. Timorousness and suspicion reinforced the harm done by undue centralization. Reflecting long afterward on his difficulties in Dublin, Newman noted in 1872: "It was not Ireland that was unkind to me. The same thing would have happened in England or France. It was the clergy, moved as they are in automation fashion from the camarilla at Rome." [19]

The principle that the Church was a communion applied to the question of papal infallibility. Shortly before the definition of 1870, Newman wrote: "The Church moves as a whole; she is not a mere philosophy; she is a communion; she not only discovers but she teaches; she is bound to consult for charity as well as for faith." The doctrine itself he had accepted on the authority of the Church when he became a Catholic. It merely added a precision about the seat of an infallibility in which bishops and faithful also shared. Already as an Anglican he held that the Church, the pillar and ground of truth, was indefectible, and before his conversion he was convinced that if Christianity was both a social and a dogmatic religion, and intended for all ages, it must have a guarantee against teaching error in essentials, which is all that the infallibility of the Church means.

After Vatican Council I Newman had to reassure many people

[19] *The Letters and Diaries of John Henry Newman,* edited by C. S. Dessain (London, 1967), p. 415; *idem, John Henry Newman,* pp. 123-27.

who were upset by the attitude of the extremists. To one friend he wrote: "Certainly the pope is not infallible beyond the deposit of faith given—though there is a party of Catholics who—I suppose to frighten away converts—wish to make out that he is giving forth infallible utterances every day." [20] He did not hide his opinion that the way the definition was forced through was scandalous, and he prophesied that it would be completed in the future. To the Anglican Alfred Plummer he wrote: "Looking at early history, it would seem as if the Church moved on to the perfect truth by various successive declarations, alternately in contrary directions, and thus perfecting, completing and supplying each other. Let us have a little faith in her, I say. Pius is not the last of the popes. The fourth Council modified the third, the fifth the fourth. . . . The late definition does not so much need to be undone as to be completed. It needs *safeguards* as to the pope's possible acts—explanations as to the matter and extent of his power. I know that if a violent reckless party had its will, it would at this moment define that the pope's power needs no safeguards, no explanations; but there is a limit to the triumph of the tyrannical. Let us be patient, let us have faith, and a new pope and a reassembled Council may trim the boat." [21]

The definition appeared to Newman potentially dangerous and in addition unnecessary. On his principles, now generally accepted, the pope can only define what the Church already believes, and in fact only once since 1870 is it certain that he has exercised his power. The definition had upset not only Catholics but others, and among them many Anglicans. Newman wrote in a letter at this time: "There was a great yearning for unity. Now apparently, it has all ceased. They seem to think it is like a child crying for the moon, a thing which cannot be."

His concern for unity was long-standing. From the time of his

[20] W. Ward, *The Life of John Henry Cardinal Newman* II (London, 1912), pp. 296 and 378. Newman's teaching is that of Vatican Council II in its *Dogmatic Constitution on the Church,* n. 25 and *Dogmatic Constitution on Divine Revelation,* n. 10.
[21] F. L. Cross, *John Henry Newman,* (London, 1933), pp. 173-74. See *Dogmatic Constitution on the Church* n. 22.

first conversion it had been the matter of his constant prayer, and it intensified as the Oxford Movement progressed. There is not room here to show how in many of his writings he was working for unity—in *Lectures on Justification*, for instance, or *Tract 90*, both of which strove to reconcile the Catholic and Protestant viewpoint, as well as in his *Letter to Pusey* and in his *Letter to the Duke of Norfolk*, which dealt with Catholic excesses concerning our Lady (to whom he had a tender devotion), and with papal infallibility respectively. All four works are important for the ecumenical dialogue today.

Newman also recognized that "the Church must be prepared for converts, as well as converts for the Church", and he regarded that preparation rather than conversions as his work. All this was a long-term operation, and various tendencies such as overcentralization, Marian exaggerations and Ultramontanism would have to be reversed. Before unity could be achieved, a common outlook was necessary. Newman realized that he had a part to play here, in view of his Anglican past, which had done so much to reanimate the Church of England. This influence might be brought to bear on Catholics. He arranged to publish a large volume of selections from his Anglican sermons, and he wrote to his editor: "I think we quite agree that the object of the selection is to cultivate a unity of ethos among those who otherwise differ." [22]

It is not possible even to mention all Newman's prophetical activities. His ecumenical work has barely been touched on. His emphasis on freedom and responsibility in education, and also in

[22] On Newman's ecumenism, see C. S. Dessain, "Cardinal Newman and Ecumenism," in *Clergy Review* (February, 1965), pp. 119-37; (March, 1965), pp. 189-206; Johannes Artz, "Newman als Brucke Zwischen Canterbury und Rom," in *Una Sancta* III (1967), pp. 173-85. The Archbishop of Canterbury said in 1966: "I am not surprised when I hear it said that the spiritual renewal of the Roman Catholic Church will involve the recapturing of some of the spirit of John Henry Newman. I believe too that the renewal of the Anglican Church will involve recapturing something of the spirit of John Henry Newman, and by that I mean . . . the recapturing of that spirit of scriptural holiness that pervades his writings from first to last": *The Rediscovery of Newman: An Oxford Symposium*, p. 8.

the religious life as exemplified in his Oratory, should be described, as well as his views on the inspiration of Scripture and on the place of the Christian in the world: "The Christian will feel that the true contemplation of his Savior lies in his worldly business." [23] In much good that he might have done, and in urgent needs he could have met, he found himself prevented from acting. This caused anguish to his pastoral soul. However, he practiced what he preached. "There is a time for everything, and many a man desires a reformation of an abuse, or the fuller development of a doctrine, or the adoption of a particular policy, but forgets to ask himself whether the right time for it has come; and, knowing that there is no one who will be doing anything toward it in his own lifetime unless he does it himself, he will not listen to the voice of authority, and he spoils a good work in his own century, in order that another man, as yet unborn, may not have the opportunity of bringing it happily to perfection in the next." [24] Newman did not make this mistake. He suffered in his lifetime, but his views have triumphed.

He resisted unbelief not for the most part by direct opposition, but positively, by trying to repair lacunae and defects in orthodoxy. Like Pope John XXIII he wished the Church to come forward to the world in all her primitive attractiveness. Both at Oxford and as a Catholic he foretold the spread of infidelity. Its fundamental dogma would be that nothing can be known for certain about the unseen world, and that it was absurd "to teach anything positively about the next world, that there is a heaven or a hell, or a last judgment, or that the soul is immortal or that there is a God". In a sermon of 1873 Newman said: "I think that the trials which lie before us are such as would appall and make dizzy even such courageous hearts as St. Athanasius, St. Gregory I or St. Gregory VII. And they would confess that, dark as the

[23] *Parochial and Plain Sermons* VIII, p. 165. Newman's papers on the religious life, edited by Dom Placid Murray, *Newman the Oratorian*, are about to be published by M. H. Gill and Son, Dublin. For inspiration, see John Henry Newman, *On the Inspiration of Scripture*, edited by J. Derek Holmes and Robert Murray, S.J., (London, 1967).
[24] *Apologia pro Vita Sua* (uniform edition), p. 259.

prospect of their own day was to them severally, ours has a darkness different in kind from any that has been before it." Belief in God would disappear—belief "in a personal God, a providence, and a moral governor". To the objection that these ideas were nothing new, he replied: "No, individuals have put them forth, but they have not been current and popular ideas. Christianity has never yet had experience of a world simply irrreligious." [25]

Who can deny that these prophecies have been in great measure verified? Newman realized vividly the force of atheism: "The world seems simply to give the lie to that great truth, the being of a God, of which my whole being is so full." "Where was the concrete representative of things invisible, which would have the force and toughness necessary to be a breakwater against the deluge?" Only in a Church "invested with the prerogative of infallibility in religious matters." "Conscience, reason, good feeling, the instincts of our moral nature, the traditions of faith and the conclusions and deductions of philosophical religion" were insufficient. "That great institution, then, the Catholic Church, has been set up by divine mercy as a present, visible antagonist, and the only possible antagonist to sight and sense." [26]

[25] "A Form of Infidelity of the Day," in *The Idea of a University* (uniform edition), pp. 388 and 393; *Catholic Sermons of Cardinal Newman*, edited at the Birmingham Oratory (London, 1957), pp. 121-23.

[26] *Apologia pro Vita Sua*, pp. 241 and 244-45; *The Idea of a University*, p. 515.

Olivier Rousseau, O.S.B./*Chèvetogne, Belgium*

Prophecy and Ecumenism

T he beginnings of the ecumenical movement in the Protestant Churches are linked with a number of great charismatic figures that appeared in the 19th century in several countries. In her lively little book about the World Student Christian Federation,[1] Suzanne de Diétrich has described the birth of several of those vocations, which an earlier historian has compared with the first group that gathered in Paris around Ignatius of Loyola, then a student in Paris.[2] First of all there was George Williams and the foundation in England toward the middle of the century of the first Christian association of young people whose object was the "evangelization of lay people by lay people and of the young by the young". A little later came the Intercollege Young Men's Christian Missions. This was followed by the Young Men's Christian Association (YMCA), founded by George Williams in 1844, and the American movement of Volunteers for the Missions, centered round John R. Mott, who occupies the central place in de Diétrich's book and who paved the way for the extraordinary development of that World Student Christian Federation which, as is well-known, was to produce the great leaders of the ecumenical

[1] *Cinquante ans d'histoire* (Paris, n.d.), p. 11; R. Rouse, *The World Student Christian Federation* (London, 1948).
[2] T. Talow, *The Story of the Student Movement of Great Britain and Ireland* (London, 1933), p. 1.

movement. The first to benefit by these movements were the missions in pagan territories, but it was also clear that here was a flowering of many positive and disinterested forces put at the service of Christ, forces which radiated in all directions.

Around 1950 the German theologian Günther Gloege started a series of monographs which he later gathered together in two volumes. They contain some seventy sketches by various authors of the main ecumenical figures of our age, whom he calls "bridge builders", and whom he situates in the perspective of the first thinkers of the Reformation.[3]

Although presented mainly in view of their actuality and not always very thoroughly, these figures gave a glimpse of the work by which the Spirit prepared the way toward unity, and they revealed in an astonishing way how the various tendencies toward unity converged throughout the world. A few Orthodox figures were also included, such as the Metropolitan Germanos of Thyatyre and Fr. Bulgakov, as well as the apostle of prayer for Christian unity, Abbé Paul Couturier of Lyons, Cardinal Bea, and another famous Catholic priest who died in a German concentration camp—a martyr in the eyes of many—Fr. F. J. Metzger, the founder of *Una Sancta*.

While Vatican Council II was in preparation, the great missiologist and ecumenist, Bishop Stephen Neill, published *Men of Unity*,[4] the cover of which carries photographs of J. R. Mott, N. Soederblom, D. T. Niles, Pope John XXIII, William Temple and

[3] *Oekumenische Profile* (Stuttgart, 1961 and 1963). Here is a revealing list of these profiles: Vol. I: J. R. Mott, W. Paton, C. H. Brent, R. H. Gardiner, R. Davidson, J. H. Oldham, G. K. A. Bell, N. Soederblom, E. Berggraf, F. Siegmund Schultze, V. Ammundsen, A. Keller, A. Deissmann, O. Dibelius, Germanos of Thyatyre, H. S. Alivisatos, S. Zankow, S. Bulgakow, Patriarchs Tykhon, Serius and Alexis of Moscow, P. Couturier, M. J. Metzger; Vol. II: S. Chakko, D. T. Niles, H. Kraemer, S. Neill, A. Schweitzer, A. Nygren, K. Barth, E. Brunner, R. Niebuhr, E. Schlink, Cardinal Bea, D. Bonhoeffer, K. Niemöller, H. Gruber, W. Menn, R. von Thadden, K. Scharf, H. Lilje, S. C. Michelfelder, B. Forell, F. Sigg, M. Boegner, P. Maury, R. Schutz, J. L. Hromadka, W. Temple, W. A. Visser 't Hooft, L. Newbigin, S. McCrea Cavert, F. C. Fry, H. Schonfeld, S. de Diétrich, M. Barot.

[4] London, 1960.

W. A. Visser 't Hooft. Appearing at that time, this book inspired a new hope and a new joy which Pope John was not afraid of describing as "a new Pentecost".

This list of publications, together with the valuable *History of the Ecumenical Movement 1517-1948* by R. R. Rouse and S. Neill [5] could easily be lengthened, but in this limited space I can but lightly touch on the main figures that fit so well together. It is rare, indeed, in the history of the Church that one can see such a fertile flowering of new and pure forces, all tending unswervingly toward the same goal, like a new pouring forth of the Spirit, and all animated by the desire to restore to the Church—the Churches—that lost unity. As the conciliar *Decree on Ecumenism* puts it: "The Lord of ages is wise and patient in the pursuit of the gracious plan that he has for us sinners. Though Christians are estranged from each other, in recent times he has begun to increase the spread among them of a heartfelt regret and longing for unity. This is a grace whose influence has been felt by men in great numbers all over the world. The grace of the Holy Spirit has encouraged the rise of a movement toward reunion among our separated brethren also, and this movement is growing daily." [6] The term "also" is a euphemism, because it is in fact among those "separated" from us that the ecumenical movement started while we were still engulfed in a night of isolation.

The words "prophecy" and "charisma" occur frequently in the books mentioned above because, as we can easily recognize today, the figures singled out by the authors were truly charismatic figures. N. Berdyaev once wrote: "The Church cannot exist without bishops and priests, whatever their human features, but deep within she lives and breathes through the saints and the prophets, the apostles and religious geniuses, the martyrs and the ascetics." [7] Such were precisely the men already referred to and those that will still be mentioned. Berdyaev himself was the "prophet of prophecy" in modern days; he had met some of the leaders of

[5] *A History of the Ecumenical Movement 1517-1948* (London, 1954).
[6] *Decree on Ecumenism*, n. 1.
[7] *De la Destination de l'Homme* (Paris, 1935), pp. 110-11.

the ecumenical movement as it took shape, particularly those of the YMCA, and he foresaw "that the age of Christian disunity was drawing to a close". His thought was that "it was not the Churches that should be approached first but the ordinary Christians. . . . Christians think that it is divine truth that separates them when, in fact, it is the human element, the psychological structure, the differences of experience, of feeling and of an intellectual kind that divide them. . . . But when we touch the root of religious reality, when we pass through a genuine spiritual experience, we come closer together and are united to Christ." [8] One night Berdyaev had a dream and he saw himself in a great gathering of the representatives of *all the Churches,* including his own: it was a Council.[9] It was a strange vision, yet it showed a reality close at hand, though unthinkable at that time.

Here one should recall that in 1925 J. R. Mott—who had always been interested in the fate of the Russians, as of all the Orthodox, within the associations to which he belonged—presided over a meeting of Russian intellectuals in Savoy which decided to found the review *Putj* (The Way). This, as Berdyaev recalled later, was "the only review that clung resolutely to the spiritual ground of Orthodoxy" [10] and its message. This review, which lasted until World War II and in which Berdyaev himself who died in 1948 played an important part, was published in Russian but had nevertheless a vast influence on the Western world because of the way in which it emphasized religious transcendence. It enjoyed the powerful cooperation of the Institute of St. Sergius of Paris, and it shows the charismatic contributions of several of its professors, including the last one to die, Fr. Nicolas Afanassieff.[11]

[8] E. Porret, *Berdiaeff, prophète des temps nouveaux* (Neuchâtel, 1931), p. 131.

[9] *Ibid.,* p. 138.

[10] *Ibid.,* p. 130.

[11] The greatest theologian of this school, endowed with great spiritual insight, was Sergius Boulgakov (d. 1944). With several professors of St. Sergius, among them Kartasev and Zenkovskij, and with other Orthodox theologians, he published in 1930, in Paris, a Russian work rich in perspectives for reunion, *La réunion chrétienne. Le problème oecu-*

Let us return to the pioneer of all this, the Methodist John Mott (1865-1955). From his very youth he gave himself totally to Christ and his work. He was a missionary of great stature, and his biographer had printed on the inside of the cover of his book two large maps of his journeys which make one think of the possible journeys of St. Paul had he lived in the 20th century.[12] Although John Mott had no influence on contemporary thought in the strict sense of the term, he nevertheless remained, as one of his main collaborators, J. H. Oldham, said when he died, "the undoubted leader of a movement which contained numerous distinguished members of the clergy and eminent professors. . . . In any practical situation he very clearly discerned what was really important. Endowed with an astonishing perception of communal experiences, [his great simplicity and integrity resulted in the fact that] when he issued a directive, practically everyone was prepared to follow it. . . . Rarely has a man exercised such an active influence and met with so little opposition".[13]

At the World Missionary Conference of Edinburgh in 1910 John Mott played a decisive part in shaping the attitude of the Churches. He had been appointed president, and people still remember an intervention of his which became famous. When a proposal was made to make the missionary activities converge toward a unification of the Protestant missions, Mott thought it necessary to set up a committee to ensure continuation. The assembly rejected it. He himself then explained the issue in such a way that it was accepted by acclamation. He said: "Let him who is against, say 'no'." There was a profound silence, followed by general hilarity.[14] The resolution was passed due to the inspiring charisma of the president, who that day unwittingly

ménique dans la conscience orthodoxe, inviting the Orthodox Churches to let their voice be heard in the ecumenical movement and not to join it too late.

[12] B. Mathews, *John Mott: World-Citizen* (London, 1934).
[13] J. H. Oldham, "John R. Mott," in *Ecumenical Review* (April, 1955), p. 259.
[14] S. Raeder, "John R. Mott, Weltstratege für planvolle christliche Zusammenarbeit," in Gloege, *Oekum. Prof.* II, p. 166.

perhaps made the Churches take a step forward toward what was to become the ecumenical movement.

There was a strangely charismatic atmosphere about this Edinburgh Conference—for example, the often quoted statement by Dr. Chang, of the Church of China, about the "isms" in which Western missionaries dress up their imported Christianity. He asked them to abandon this line and "to allow Jesus Christ himself to raise up a Church among the Asiatic peoples corresponding to the character of the race".[15] This formula became decisive for that other prophet of ecumenism, Bishop Charles Brent (1852-1929), who, on his return to America, decided at the Conference of Cincinnati, with the help of his friend, R. H. Gardiner, to start a movement which would put an end to the baneful divisions among Christians. This was, without doubt, a fresh call of the Spirit which was to lead to the movement of Faith and Order. The two pioneers set up a delegation which visited all the Church leaders after the war of 1914-18. It had been preceded by an active correspondence with the leaders of the Protestant, Orthodox and Catholic Churches. They visited Athens, Constantinople, Sofia, Bucharest, Belgrade, Rome, Alexandria, Jerusalem, Damascus, Paris, London, Norway and Sweden. At the Phanar, in 1919, the Greek metropolitans wasted no time during the vacancy of the patriarchal See caused by the Greco-Turkish war, and they drafted an encyclical on the unity of Christians which was issued in 1920.[16] Last October, in Geneva, Dr. Visser 't Hooft recalled this event in the presence of Patriarch Athenagoras,[17] who was present at the arrival of the American delegation in Athens, in 1919, while he was still a deacon and secretary to the archbishop of Athens. He was profoundly moved by that meeting which decided his ecumenical attitude, the unexpected consequences of which have become evident in recent years. He, too, became a prophet of ecumenism

---

[15] M. Boegner, *loc. cit.,* p. 40; cf. M. Villain, *Introduction à l'Oecuménisme* (Paris, 1964), p. 19.

[16] O. Rousseau, "L'Orthodoxie et le mouvement oecuménique," in *Ephem. Theol. Lov.* (1967), p. 172; *Istina* (1955), p. 93.

[17] *Irénikon* (1967), p. 537.

when, at the election of Pope John XXIII, he said to the new pope: "A man was sent by God, and his name was John." Soon after 1919 the founders of Faith and Order met Archbishop Soederblom of Uppsala (1866-1931) in Geneva, who had initiated the movement of Life and Work. His idea to bring together the Church leaders, even of the countries involved in World War I, in 1917 was then thought of as utopian and naïve. Nevertheless, Dr. Visser 't Hooft could say recently: "At this distance we may say that we have to be profoundly grateful that there was a man, a great Christian, who saved the Church's honor during that first world war when so many 'preachers presented arms' " (this was the title of a book which appeared in America after the war).[18]

In 1919, at Wassenaar, Holland, Soederblom read this sentence from his diary: "I propose the setting up of an ecumenical council which shall be the spiritual representation of Christianity and which shall provide a common approach to this Christianity." As this suggestion was judged premature, he added: "Even if I cannot yet have a genuine ecumenical council, I can at least organize a major conference." [19] It was indeed too early to join Faith and Order with Life and Work; the supporters of the first wished to maintain their independence, but Soederblom's idea made headway. It was not that he was opposed, as has been said, to a doctrinal agreement among Christians. "My task is already so difficult," he said, "that if I tie up my conference on practical questions with theological and doctrinal issues, I shall not have a chance of achieving anything at all." [20]

The Conference on Life and Work took place at Stockholm in 1925; it celebrated the commemoration of the Council of Nicea of 325, 1,600 years after the event. Among those present were the Orthodox, especially Patriarch Photios of Alexandria, who recited the creed of the first councils in Greek. After the Conference on Faith and Order in 1927 at Lausanne, Pius XI pub-

[18] W. A. Visser 't Hooft, "Nathan Soederblom, figure de prophète du Mouvement Oecuménique," in *Oecumenica* II (Strasbourg, 1967), p. 139.
[19] *Ibid.*, p. 140.
[20] *Ibid.*, p. 145.

lished his famous encyclical *Mortalium animos* in 1929, which had been ready for two years, and which was largely directed against Soederblom, who was profoundly upset by it. Dr. Visser 't Hooft has related how, in 1929, after a discussion of this encyclical, Soederblom had exclaimed: "Church history tells us that when Rome has spoken, the case is concluded: *causa finita est*. But in fact, when Rome has spoken it is far from concluded. It is only just beginning." [21] This was a truly prophetic word when one thinks of what has happened in our own days.

Soederblom's dream gradually took shape until in 1948, at Amsterdam, with the help of Karl Barth, the movements of Faith and Order and Life and Work were merged in a single ecumenical council to which, within a short time, 200 Churches adhered. In 1961 the Missionary Conference was also incorporated at New Delhi. The dogmatic formula, which until then had been a christological one, now became trinitarian; the Orthodox joined in vast numbers, and for the first time there was an official delegation of Catholic observers.

No doubt, the growing institutionalization would in the long run create a danger for the council, whose antecedents were above all charismatic. Nevertheless, the fact remains that the breath of the Spirit can hover over the institution without being affected by it. If the increasing membership of Churches and related issues could create a fear of spiritual impoverishment in the World Council, the growing convergence toward unity and the accelerated pace of this process may also well be the work of the Spirit who keeps his charisms alive, even if people notice it less.

It is true that today the World Council is reaching a point which makes one worry because of the widespread doctrinal upheaval and the pressure of problems which beset the world. It is to be hoped that the next conference at Uppsala in July 1968 will revive the memory of Soederblom, his prophetic dynamism and his movement after the stages it has been through during the

[21] *Ibid.*, p. 145.

last forty years, and will not let the flame be snuffed out. After all, behind all this God is at work.

During all the time that the first phases of the ecumenical movement developed, the Catholic Church could only point to individuals who, here and there, under a cloud of mistrust and skepticism, worked as solitary pioneers at their own risk and peril. It is a pity that I can only give here the names of those that died; the list of those that are living would be too long. We must mention first of all Cardinal Mercier (1851-1926) who, together with Lord Halifax (1839-1934) and Abbé Portal (d. 1926), started the famous Malines Conversations. These were frowned upon at the time by the English Catholics, but they opened a way and a question was raised. Mercier said one day that the audacity lay in knowing how far one can go before he goes too far. He often put this original view into practice. His exceptional qualities gave him an extraordinary clear insight in Church affairs and were recently described in these words: "The true stature of a man is not measured by the size of the generations that come after him, and who now all think as he did, but by the age when he lived and when he did not think like everyone else." [22] Certainly, Mercier did not think like everyone else. He was far-sighted, and he ennobled everything he touched. In his contacts with the first Russian emigrants as with the Anglicans that came to Malines, he was free from all formalism. In a pastoral letter he wrote: "Under no circumstances would I let a separated brother say that he knocked hopefully on the door of a Roman Catholic bishop and that this bishop refused to open. . . . I would consider myself guilty if I ever were so cowardly." [23] He not only opened the door but the whole grandeur of his soul and pastoral genius. It is often said that the conversations between Mercier and Halifax produced nothing concrete. It remains true, as Abbé Portal has said, that "at that moment the religious atmosphere of England changed". The mixed Commissions of the

[22] E. Beauduin, *Le Cardinal Mercier* (Tournai, 1966), p. 109.
[23] "Lettre pastorale à son clergé du 18 janvier 1924 sur les Conversations de Malines," in *Irénikon Collection* II, p. 76.

Secretariat for Unity with the Anglican Church, which had their last meeting in Malta in January 1968, are in a certain sense a resumption of those conversations in a more favorable climate.

Together with Cardinal Mercier we must mention Dom Lambert Baudouin (1873-1960) who founded a monastery for Christian unity at Amay (later transferred to Chèvetogne). The famous memoir he presented at the Malines Conversations, with its prophetic title, "The Anglican Church United, not Absorbed", created a great stir, and almost a scandal, at the time, but would today fit in very well with the pluralist outlook of the ecclesiology of Vatican Council II, at least in its main approach. Dom Baudouin's great intuition was twofold. First, he thought that those who wanted to work for Christian unity should reverse the tactics of individual conversions while advocating as essential the psychological approach, which today we call the "dialogue method". Second, he saw that it was necessary to establish contact with all the separated Churches without exception. Thus his work led up to the conciliar *Decree on Ecumenism* and to the work of the Secretariat for Unity, embracing not only the East which had held most attention at the start, but the great ecumenical movement inaugurated in 1925, the date of the foundation of his monastery. In any case, the Eastern Orthodox had not stood aside from ecumenism at that time when in the Catholic Church, and particularly in Rome, the tendency was to go in the opposite direction. Dom Baudouin had a great deal to suffer because of this twofold approach embodied in his program. From 1929 to 1951 he lived in exile away from his monastery, and he had to leave the continuation of his work to a young and not yet fully formed community in the hope that it would not change course. This work was done in large part by its review *Irénikon*.

He was a personal friend of John XXIII, whom he had often met and with whom he had stayed on his travels in the East, and while he was still patriarch of Venice, Baudouin heard him pay this unexpected tribute one day at a Congress at Palermo in 1957: "The main flaw in the work for unity is that it is not sufficiently propagated among the mass of the people who would nevertheless be capable of appreciating it. My old Belgian friend, Dom Lambert Baudouin, said in 1926 when I was still at the beginning of my practical task of cooperation in the Near East: 'For the reunion of the separated Churches we must create in the West a movement parallel to that of the propagation of the faith.' " Within a few years after Vatican Council II, and particularly since the meetings between Paul VI and Athenagoras, this movement has grown astonishingly throughout the Catholic Church, and has perhaps reached the same degree of zeal and intensity as that of the missionary movement.

When Pius XII died, Dom Baudouin, with his clear view of things, had already said that the choice would be Cardinal Roncalli, and he added: "I know him; the first thing he will do is to summon a Council for reunion." If this statement had not been repeated several times and had not been reported by different witnesses, one might not believe it. The morning after the Council had been announced, on January 26, 1959, he said to one of his intimate friends: "You will see; it is going to happen: unity." He died too soon (January 1960) to see the beginning of the vindication of his great prophecy, but, judging by what has happened since then, even if only seven years afterward, the events have not failed to prove him true. He was not only a pioneer of the liturgical movement and of work for Christian unity in the Catholic Church, but he had also paved the way through his studies for that development in the theology of episcopacy which emerged at the Council.[24]

Another outstanding apostle of unity, Abbé Paul Couturier (1881-1953), came to spend a month at Amay in 1932 in order to penetrate himself with what he called "the spiritual testament of Cardinal Mercier". This has been summarized as follows: "To unite one must love; to love one must know one another; to know one another one must meet one another." He applied this

[24] O. Rousseau, "Pioneri dell' apostolato unionistico: Dom Lambert Baudouin," in *Oriente Cristiano* (April, 1965), p. 77.

formula literally. Throughout his life he exercised a discreet but profound influence, had the humility of a saint, and was totally dedicated to prayer and his relations with non-Catholics. His death revealed his stature, and today the part he played as an apostle of unity is known by all through the book of M. Villain [25] for Catholics, and that of G. Curtis [26] for Anglicans. His name is identified by the new formula of the prayer for unity, which has been accepted by all the Churches and respects every kind of ecclesiology; it is to pray for the visible unity of all Christians "such as Christ wants it and by the means he shall choose." At first this formula was severely criticized, but today it has been adopted as the official theme of Unity Week each January by all denominations and has been accepted by the World Council of Churches. Paul Couturier was the great pioneer of the week of prayer in this new way. Through it he reached a vast number of Christians by an influence beyond human effort; he was visibly supported by God.

This list is too short, because it is too early for such work as that of Gloege about Catholic workers for reunion; one might mention several other names—for instance, Metropolitan Szepticky (d. 1944)—as belonging to the previous generation. He was the friend of Vladimir Soloviev whose insights, perhaps somewhat out-of-date today, nevertheless announced better days in his time. And for our own generation there is the Melkite Patriarch Maximos IV (d. 1967), who was one of the leading figures at the Council. I would also like to add the name of Dom Clement Lialine who was, for a long time, editor of *Irénikon*, and who died at the age of 56 in 1958.[28] His passion for unity and his penetrating mind showed the way to many others. Among the living the only one whom shortage of space allows us to mention is Fr. Congar, whose ecumenical career and indefat-

[25] *L'Abbé Paul Couturier, apôtre de l'Unité Chrétienne* (Tournai, 1959).

[26] *Paul Courturier and Unity* (London, 1964).

[27] Archbishop of Leopol in Galicia, a friend of Cardinal Mercier and one of the great figures of unity between the two world wars. Cf. *Irénikon* (1946), p. 49.

[28] Cf. *Irénikon* (1958), p. 165.

igable labors for the Church are charismatically inspired. His friends will forgive me for not making the list any longer.

It will be remembered that at the beginning of the Council, on October 20, 1962, the fathers published a message to the world which recalled on more than one point the program envisaged by Soederblom and his Life and Work movement. It was said then that this message did not correspond to the doctrinal purpose envisaged during the preparation for the Council. Although it was proclaimed in the general assembly and published, it was not incorporated in the *acta* of the Council because it was said to reflect only partly the opinion of the fathers and because the pope had only tacitly agreed to it. Nevertheless, at the beginning of the second session Paul VI gave it its full value and compared it with the witness of St. Peter and the other apostles on the day of Pentecost. Thus it prepared the way for Schema XIII on the Church in the modern world, a schema which created and still creates a great stir, and has not failed to affect the trend of affairs in the World Council of Churches. The Spirit can also raise storms, and nothing prevents us from seeing in this one of his new creative interventions. All we have so quickly surveyed here shows that the wind of change which has blown over the Churches for sixty years is, in spite of all denominational differences, a homogeneous force beyond the power of man. The work of John XXIII, conciliar encounters between Catholic bishops and non-Catholic observers, the mutual visits of Church leaders and the contacts that are taking place in "mixed groups" have been, and still are, a powerful illustration of this point.

In the present circumstances, and on the threshold of the Uppsala Conference, we might remember that the conciliar aggiornamento, desired by Pope John, bore no doubt on the Church *ad intra,* in herself, but still more on the Church *ad extra,* in her relations with the world outside. All that is happening in various milieus, and that may look like the appearing of cracks in the edifice, is, so to speak, the necessary reverse of ecumenism. As Cardinal Bea said when he welcomed Patriarch Athenagoras to the audience at the Vatican, the post-conciliar aggiornamento is "the basic condition for progress on the way toward unity". If there is some disintegration today at various levels in the life of the Churches, and if this sometimes frightens the faithful, let us think of the first words of the conciliar *Decree On ecumenism: unitatis redintegratio. Reintegration* and *disintegration* go together and influence each other. The data of the faith and the order of the Church must seek to create a new harmony, difficult to establish, and here the work of men and their imperfections are the necessary accompaniment of God's work.

In conclusion I would like to mention a last point which seems also due to a prophetic charism. The great apostle of unity in the years 1910-1924, R. Gardiner, who has been mentioned several times in this article, wrote in November 1914 a letter on Christian Unity to Cardinal Gasparri, then Secretary of State to Benedict XV. This letter, written in impeccable Latin, was reproduced in 1919 by M. Pribilla, S. J. in his book *Um Kirchliche Enheit.*[29] It contained the following astonishing sentence, perhaps inspired by the writings of Leo XIII: "We ardently wish that the Church of Rome which has always vindicated the need of restoring Christian unity (*quae redintegrandae unitatis vindicem semper sese praebuit*) may assist us in our efforts"— namely, the Conference on Faith and Order which was then planned. Those words, *redintegrandae unitatis,* are precisely those chosen to open the *Decree on Ecumenism* of Vatican Council II, exactly fifty years later in November 1964, *unitatis redintegratio;* they were already used by Paul VI and will remain in history the name by which this Decree is known.

[29] Munich, 1929, p. 314; in *Irénikon* 1 (1967), I have dealt more extensively with the curious antecedents of this letter.

Albert Sohier, S.A.M./*Brussels, Belgium*

Père Vincent Lebbe: Prophet and Missionary

I f the prophet is primarily one who is entrusted with the Word of God, then surely missionary activity is eminently prophetic. This fact is singularly well illustrated in this century by a man whose whole life was devoted to the missions—Père Vincent Lebbe (born in Ghent in 1877; died in Chunking in 1940).

The focal interest of his varied activity was to bring the Word of life into the hearts of men. Few men must have spoken as much as he—if one includes his letters. Personally he was charming. This is how Fr. van der Meer from Walcheren in The Netherlands described him: "His face . . . would light up, and he would become quite attractive when he spoke of the Chinese, the 'cream of souls' as he called them. . . . All he could speak of was souls and the wonders of grace. The truly Gospel simplicity in the way he spoke showed a burning compassion and a pure shining love. . . ."

His attitude during the great crisis of his life (1916-1919) was typical of him. Under pressure from the French "protectorate", he was moved at first from Tientsin to Chengtung; far from relaxing or resting in order to begin again, and even further from feeling bitter, he launched an apostolate among the neighboring pagans as far as Shunteh with the encouragement of Msgr. de

Vienne, his former co-worker who was vicar apostolic of Cheng-tung at that time. Sent eventually to the far corners of his own vicariate, he brought about an educational congress to put the Church into contact with the forward-looking elements of that region. Then, at the critical stage, he was removed to the south. When he arrived there his principal trial was ignorance of the local dialect which prevented him from telling the news about Christ. The words of St. Paul—"Woe to me if I do not preach the Gospel"—Père Lebbe made his own throughout his life. This concern is the heart of that action by which he "prophetically" prepared for the development of the Church of Jesus Christ in China and beyond: Asiatic and African bishops, suppression of foreign "protection", national emancipation, social questions, the meaning of Scripture, liturgical reform, encouragement of lay responsibility, teaching and study groups, the press, respect for non-Christian religions and ecumenism. During all this ac-tion, which he himself freely described as revolutionary, he was —paradoxically?—deeply attached to the Church and to a tra-dition: that of the saints.

In the thick of the struggle he wrote to his intimate friend and fellow-fighter Père Antoine Cotta, at that time recovering in Tientsin: "If Rome should criticize my ideas or actions, even though on the face of it it would seem to be the result of a multitude of human, very human, plots and counterplots, of poli-tics, *combinazioni,* etc., nevertheless I would fully submit myself, body and soul, and cheerfully too, believing that everything is for the best, at least for now, believing that my obedience will be good both for myself and *for everybody.* For that which is most real in affairs is not that which is the most obvious. God and his grace are at work, too. . . . I would wish to be with the saints, to keep close to them, and in this way to follow the path beaten out by the great ones among these truly wise men. Nevertheless, one must clearly make the reservation that one must try (if the terms of the condemnation permit, and to the extent that a true inter-pretation will permit, no more) to obtain from Rome help to realize the plans I consider necessary for the Church in China".

Such a passage has many fellows. This faithfulness had become rooted in him when, at the beginning of 1908 after the condemnation of "modernism", he overcame a profound dark night of faith. His commitment to his missionary vocation was to lead at last to some kind of definitive illumination.

The "Sign" of the Prophetic Mission

Père Lebbe knew that his "prophetic" attitude, without the charism of a hierarchic function, could lead to the demand for a "sign". His unshakeable loyalty was indeed a sign in itself. In addition, one could add the ending of his remarkable letter of September 18, 1917 to Msgr. Reynaud, vicar apostolic of Ningpo and doyen of the Chinese bishops: "And I have no sign, other than that I have suffered; and also that I do not think that in all that I have done I have ever acted for a human ideal; rather, I have been accompanied by . . . the sign of witnesses who in speaking have all to lose and nothing to gain."

Such a sign was rather that of a Jeremiah than a "sign of Jonah". Later there were to be signs of another kind, in our opinion. In July 1918 there was the sudden cure of a nun of Shaohing about to die of tuberculosis. The story appeared with episcopal approval in the *Little Messenger of Ningpo*. There was also the "inexplicable" cure of a Chinese student in Louvain in 1925. Nor can one omit mention of the series of "coincidences" in his life: the consecration of the first Chinese bishops on the jubilee day of his priesthood; his death on the feast of St. John the Baptist, patron of his Little Brothers; the eve of Passion Sunday (1917: exiled from the vicariate of Tientsin; 1927: arrival at Ankwo after his return to China; 1940: capture by the communists). However, it is now time to consider the call of God.

Vocation

Freddy (for such was his baptismal name) Lebbe was only a child when the "life" of the Blessed J. G. Perboyre, a martyr in China, indicated for him his future road. (His personal reminiscences say he was five or six years old; his Benedictine brother thinks he was about eleven.) Soon his family knew. Nevertheless the final decision was painful as he remembered later: "While I was admiring the beautiful spring countryside, suddenly my thoughts opened up, so to speak; I felt an absolute mission to go to China weighing upon me. 'Lord, must I really go to China? How painful it will be to leave my relatives and my native land to go to distant China. What will I do there?' But I really had the idea that I had been given an order to go there."

While studying theology his health seemed to suggest that providence wished otherwise. At that time (July 8, 1899) he wrote to his brother: "What will be my life's goal, Lord! At least let me not follow too far behind the voice I have heard since childhood, and may it involve crosses—I deserve the cross!" He did not wish to pursue higher studies at Rome, for that would exclude missionary work, and he was completely sure of his "missionary vocation". And yet he would discuss Hebrew (in which he used to write on postcards), Greek, Syriac and Arabic with his brother. Then in the autumn of 1900 he found himself in the Eternal City. But while his friend and co-worker Paul Dehocq was writing to Dom Bede: "I believed in Freddy's vocation despite his pessimism" (January 23, 1901), Msgr. Favier, vicar apostolic of Peking and "hero" of the seige of Petang in 1900, chose him, against all odds, for his own diocese.

His specific future role was far from obvious to him. "When I left for China I knew *nothing,* absolutely nothing of what awaited me apart from the essential: that I was going 'ad gentes' ", was his accurate comment in 1928. In fact, in coming to China he had said: "Here am I who have made myself a missionary in a French congregation in order to make France loved. . . ." Moreover, in the midst of the aftermath of the Dreyfus affair, he had praised an anti-Semitic work by Drumond and had filled in an odd corner of a postcard with: "Long live France! Down with the Yids!" One scarcely expects such a man to be a future champion of the equality of races! His letters on the trip also were studded with phrases like: "One loves France more than ever" (February 18, 1901); "Long live France" (February 20, 1901) and at Djibouti: "The precious flag" (February 24, 1901). And this was a Belgian!

This corner of Africa also gave him "the wish to do good to these poor people whom one can surely win by kindness and lose by hardness and injustice. I have seen things here which make my heart bleed—and even from priests. I know well that I will have to suffer much. . . ." Each stage of his journey from then on gave him the same feeling: Colombo, Saigon, Hongkong (where he added a recognition of Chinese superiority). At Shanghai he appreciated the Boxer Rebellion; he felt that 99% of the wrongs were on the European side. On the eve of his ordination Vincent Lebbe made plain to Msgr. Jarlin the new line of action his conscience would impose: not to accommodate himself to the false position of the Church in China. Then, on January 19, 1902, when he left as a true missionary, he said clearly: "I am no longer French."

Was there perhaps some psychological basis for such a change? From 1899, it is true, he had emphasized his "democratic" (or social) convictions which he saw as based upon justice. And on July 13, 1901, he had written: "How the democratic soul of dear Stephen would suffer if he were to see how a people is crushed because its color is different from ours and its civilization a little backward. . . ." Yet the speed, decision and the special apostolic and spiritual nature of the transformation show the work of grace and a special call. And how long we had to wait for similar ideas from *Populorum progressio!*

African and Asian Episcopate

Space is lacking for even a brief statement of this vital activity of Père Lebbe. His work is dealt with at greater length elsewhere,[1] and we will content ourselves with underlining and adding some special aspects of his work.

[1] J. Leclercq, *Thunder in the Distance* (New York, 1958); P. Goffert and A. Sohier, *Lettres du Père Lebbe* (Paris-Tournai, 1960) (see especially the index under "clergé autochtone").

Since 1908 he had extolled the merits of a "fully native clergy" for China, but in his plea of 1917 he had enlarged his perspective and noted how odd it was that the only way in which the Japanese were treated as unequal was on this question. At the end of 1918 or early in 1919 he had the comfort to read articles in the *Catholic Herald of India* where Père Gille espoused the same cause for India.

Then, after an overlong delay in Père Lebbe's opinion, Msgr. Costantini named the two first prefects apostolic—without episcopal character—at the end of 1923 and the beginning of 1924. The missionary felt here the effects of a movement to prevent a native episcopate, for apart from the difficult territories assigned to them, he knew the defects of character of Msgr. Souen. (They led in fact to his eventual forced dismissal, fortunately late enough not to harm the general policy, although Père Lebbe had enough to suffer personally in consequence between 1930 and 1936.)

In 1925 in Brussels Père Lebbe met Père Gille who had been exiled to India because of his "subversive" views. With the encouragement of Cardinal Mercier, the editor of the *Revue Catholique des Ideés et des Faits* published two articles on the episcopacy in India. The vigorous reaction provoked from Pius XI the encyclical *Rerum ecclesiae;* then soon after Paul Staes, a layman from Liège, had pleaded Père Lebbe's cause in Rome, orders were given on March 30, 1926 for the episcopal consecration of Philip Tchao, who was first on a list submitted by the missionary at the end of 1920.

Following the consecration of six more Chinese bishops on October 28, 1926, Père Lebbe was under the impression that 30 to 40 more would be nominated in the next few years. This proved to be a false hope. There were not that number ten years after his death! Nevertheless the movement, once launched, gained support and affected Japan, India, Vietnam, Uganda and Madagascar before his death; it then spread throughout Asia and Africa, giving an almost truly universal character to Vatican Council II.

Emancipation from Foreign "Protection"

For the Church to be rooted in China demanded the suppression of French "protection", and here too Père Lebbe exercised his "prophetic" role.

We have recently shown [2] the extent to which the foreign concessions lacked legal foundation, harmed the preaching of the Gospel and were of doubtful material advantage. It was not until 1918, it would seem, that Père Lebbe was fully conscious of this absence of foundation (he does not rule it out, for instance, in his letter to Msgr. Reynaud in 1917), although, as we have seen, he recognized its harmful effects during his first year in China.

In 1908, scarcely yet installed in the Center for International Relations in Tientsin, he forsaw a nuncio for China. It was precisely in 1916, when the French diplomats realized his disapproval of their behavior, that the storm broke over him. But this led him, together with his friend Cotta, to try to make Rome throw off all foreign patronage. At the same time he approached Ma Siang-Po (an important Catholic political figure, and an ex-Jesuit) and René Lou Tseng-siang, the Minister for Foreign Affairs (also a Catholic and later a Benedictine monk of Saint André, Bruges). This resulted in an ephemeral diplomatic link being formed between China and the Holy See in 1918 (Msgr. Petrelli as nuncio).

When France and her "allies" had forced China to retreat and the latter had abandoned relations with the Holy See, Père Lebbe insisted that a "delegate for the Church alone" be sent. On his return to Europe, he spoke of this problem with Cardinal Gaspari, Secretary of State, on December 27, 1920. A year and a half later Msgr. Costantini, who was sent in a quasi-clandestine manner, took as his secretary Philip Tchao, a friend of Père Lebbe. From then on the influence of the "protectorate" lessened until diplomatic relations were recognized between China and the Vatican in 1943.

[2] *Nouvelle Revue de Science Missionaire* (Schöneck/Beckzenried, 1967), pp. 226-283.

Let us recall briefly the previous attempts. From 1881 until 1886 Msgr. Raimondi from Hongkong and Msgr. Volonteri from Honan, opposed by Msgr. Favier and the French government, had led a campaign with this objective and with due care for the dignity of their position. But the contemporary maneuvers of the Italian Franciscans, of Msgr. Anzer, and later of the "Belgian missions" were concerned also, if not primarily, with fostering the political and commercial schemes of other governments. Père Lebbe, on the other hand, a true "prophet" and a person of importance (he was also vicar general from 1914-1917, although this was purely nominal from June 1916), had completely unmixed motives. For he had never denied his sympathy for France, other than for China's benefit. He was totally on her side in 1914-1918; this was reflected in his newspaper *I Shih Pao* (People's Welfare Daily), and Msgr. Henninghaus, S.V.D., vicar apostolic of Yenchow, Shantung, indicated that he could not support him openly, his own roots being in Catholic Germany. Nevertheless, immediately after the armistice, Père Lebbe used all his influence with Rome and in China to prevent the expulsion of the German Missionaries.

Social Action

In certain circumstances at least a missionary's secondary activities are undoubtedly also "prophetic". This was the case with Père Lebbe's social role.

Let us leave aside his charitable actions, heroic and frequent though they undoubtedly were. For in addition he kept up the "democratic" enthusiasm of his youth to the extent that his last message (at the beginning of 1940)—the annotated Rule for his Little Brothers—had the following directive: "Save men, save the whole man, *body* and soul."

After the 1911 revolution, a professor of sociology was needed at the new school for administrative sciences in Tientsin, and Père Lebbe was asked to accept the position; he took it in his stride and 20,000 copies of his course were printed and used! This is his comment in 1933: "True, we must make preparation with all our strength, but we must not shrink from a risk; one must be sure that since God has given the chance he will also give his grace and even a kind of comfort."

In his daily paper *I Shih Pao,* from October 1915 he gave a weekly social chronicle until, less than a year later, his superiors forbade all collaboration. With the spread of a social doctrine of Christian inspiration interrupted in this way, the field was free for a Marxist one which, if we are to believe Mao Tse-Tung himself, did not really begin to spread in China and affect him until after the Bolshevik revolution in October 1917.

Practically speaking, quite apart from the general approach of his first period in the Wu-ts'ing-hsien (1902-1905), he brought about an "employment agency" in Tientsin for Christians fresh from the country. On the basis of a workers' study group, he thought of beginning a trade union. He suggested that such unions should be founded at Tangshan, beyond his own vicariate and the center of the collieries of the Kailan Mining Administration, but the missionary on the spot did not know what to make of the suggestion. In the Summer of 1918 Père Lebbe was arbitrator between management and workers in Shaohing.

From 1920-1927, while in Europe, he was also interested in the workers; a notebook with his comments on the subject has been preserved. Despite his other crushing occupations he gave catechism instruction in Billancourt; often he obtained for some person or other a job or a bed in a hospital. He also wished for a social formation for the students who were his special responsibility. They were sent to study with Marius Gonin, to the "Chronique sociale" and to Lyons. Each year several were dispatched to the French Social Week.

On his return to China he encouraged the formation of a mutual loan society for farmers, and only the difficult conditions prevalent during those days prevented a considerable extension of this scheme.

Since 1906 Père Lebbe had wished that the monasteries would keep some kind of model farm and teach even the pagans "the latest agricultural techniques". Later he gave the same mission, in the more general sense of working to raise the living standards of the masses, to his Little Brothers, telling them to live on the level of the poor peasants and workers where they resided.

Lay People and Catholic Action

The facts already given imply a particular attitude to the laity. From the first, while still in the country, he had loved to argue at length with his "catechists", responsible lay members of the Christian community. Arriving at the end of 1906 to be "director" at Tientsin, he was even more inclined to let Christians sit when visiting him, to invite them to meals and to object to the fact that they made a prostration before priests; all of this made him the object of complaints, even in writing, to his superior, Msgr. Jarlin.

Heads of households were asked to form financial boards to support the parish schools. Then he organized a Catholic Action association. Blessed with the facility for getting things started, he next initiated the national congresses for Catholic Action in Tientsin in 1912 and 1914. From distant Szechwan, Msgr. Chouvellon sent people to find out about this "Tientsin method"; finally, on December 20, 1916, he wrote to Père Lebbe: "You are doing too much good; Satan must interfere; you are persecuted for justice and truth." On February 21, 1917, he wrote to Cotta: "I heartily approve of M. Lebbe, who I know is persecuted".

Other bishops and religious superiors at first supported the movement and his papers, but soon tenacious opposition—as Msgr. Constantini still noted in 1928, although not without unfavorable comment—underlined its "prophetic" nature. In this way opportunities were missed.

Schools and Students

Director of the district of Cho-Chow in 1905-1906, Père Lebbe, seeing that China desired modern education, wished to establish a normal school ("technical college"), the first of its kind in the north. Of necessity, he himself had to take charge of the mathematics course. He aroused among the laity, even among the non-Christians, a movement to support him. However, Msgr. Jarlin was not enthusiastic; he wished only for schools for catechumens. To him the rest were castles in the air and petitions of the faithful, though most respectful, represented Protestantism, to be frowned on as comparable with the condemned *associations cultuelles* favored by the anti-clerical governments in France.

Having established primary schools in Tientsin, Père Lebbe sought to establish schools for higher education, and also for girls. This was one of the goals of his journey to Europe in 1913 which would not have been so unsuccessful had it not been for the war. Yet the foundation of Fu-Yen University in 1925 was at root the result of the impulse given at that time by Père Lebbe. Soon after the war and the famous demonstration of May 4, 1919 in Peking, he understood that the Chinese future was going to be determined by the outlook of these students. Within the narrow limits of the possible and stateable, he set himself to advocate a double approach: to the Chinese students abroad and to the non-Catholic universities in China itself. He set out these ideas to Msgr. de Guébriant, vicar apostolic of Canton (future superior general of the Paris Foreign Missions) who completed the apostolic visitation with which he had been entrusted by the Holy See by assigning him to Shanghai with this object. An occasion was found to send him back to Europe.

Lack of space forces us to refer once again to an article we have written for further details of these developments in the work for foreign students.[3] There it is shown that Père Lebbe could be considered the instigator of all the Church's work for Asiatic and African students in Europe, and even in America. But the cost was high, for since his Paris superiors wished to use him for other work than this, which they had not given him to do, they did not support him and instead gave him another appointment. His zeal soon caused him to be doing the work of at least

[3] *Annuaire missionaire catholique de la Suisse 1959* (Fribourg, 1959), pp. 31-36.

three men. So for the largest part of this period Père Lebbe did not sleep for more than several hours *a week* (and that often on the floor), apart from a restricted period on the train, or in the corner of a waiting room, or at some friend's home. His sense of dedication was an exceptional gift of which he was aware. One night the curate Boland de Verviers wanted to stay up with him to help with his uncontrollable correspondence; Père Lebbe gently told him: "No, go to sleep; you have not the grace for that." The next day the curate found him still at work. Not that he found this easy: "If it were not for you," he exclaimed one day to the crucifix, "I certainly would not do it!"

His generous apostolic spirit is to be seen also in his efforts to revive German Catholicism. In this, he did not hesitate to approach Dr. Sonnenschein, chaplain to the Berlin students, although he could not possibly have been ignorant of the fact that this ecclesiastic had fled from the Rhineland when it was occupied by the Belgian army because of his activity in encouraging and organizing traitors (as it must have seemed to him) in Belgium during the war, while Père Lebbe's family, which was so dear to him, had suffered so much during the German invasion.

The Press

Concern for the widest possible diffusion of the Christian message led Père Lebbe to an interest in the press. Apart from previous efforts, in 1911 he transplanted, fostered and established a small parish magazine at Tientsin which he had first helped Père Selinka to start in the country. This was the weekly *Kuang I Lu* (Public Benefit Record) which soon earned him the wrath of Msgr. Jarlin who was disturbed by the boldness of the initiative. Fortunately, the formation of a vicariate in Tientsin cut short any countermeasures.

In 1915 he launched *I Shih Pao* (People's Welfare Daily), the first Catholic daily in the Far East; the weekly version became the *Sunday People's Welfare,* and soon there was also a weekly woman's magazine, the first of its kind in China. He was planning a publication for the clergy when his great crisis occurred.

He founded two periodicals in Europe to foster his work, one in Chinese and one in French. After 1937, he had a paper, first at Ankwo and then later in the mountains at T'ai-hang-shan. He wanted to write books as well. No one has studied this aspect of his work sytematically to date, but here are some examples. In August 1918 he had in the stocks a pamphlet on confession, instructions for catechists, and a life of the Curé of Ars. Among the students in Europe he tried to convince some to become translators and Catholic writers, and in 1925 he proposed a project to Msgr. Constantini for a Catholic publishing house which would be a real asset in China; this would have preceded by 20 years the Catholic Central Bureau formed on the eve of the communist victory—too late despite the good work it would do. Later he was to dream of important developments in the printing world for his Little Brothers.

Holy Scripture

Among Pére Lebbe's writings was his Chinese translation of St. Paul, carried out during the 1914-1918 war. For this he searched out old texts in the British Museum and made use of the work of Morrison, the Protestant pioneer in this field. This was no amateur's work. Certainly, apart from his "temptation" to study, it was always the Bible and especially St. Paul that had an attraction for him. At one time he had even taken a professor's place with real skill; this was before his ordination when he had to run a course in Scripture in Peking.

In this way Père Lebbe was "for his period" (that of Père Lagrange whom he admired) the precursor for China. If his work was published in Chekiang in mid-1919, as it would seem to have been, circumstances did not favor its diffusion. It was twenty years before there was a modern Catholic edition of the New Testament and a start had been made on a scientific translation of the whole Bible.

His absorption with the Bible was probably unusual for the period. In his correspondence, however hasty or personal, one finds incessant quotations—or better, reminiscences—from

Scripture such as are to be found in St. Bernard. He was not so much a scholar as one who lived the scriptures.

Liturgy

Liturgically, too, Père Lebbe showed himself "up to date". As a seminarian he lived through the liturgical renewal and spread the Gregorian Chant of Solesmes.

As early as his first trip to China in 1901 he had hinted at ideas which he was later to develop in a letter to Dom Lambert Baudouin (January 15, 1914). When published, this letter became the first public defense (45 years before Vatican Council II) of a liturgy in a living language.

In 1928 he adapted the Office for his Little Brothers into Chinese, with *ad hoc* melodies. It was a similar insight which inspired him to accept natural Chinese names for baptism and really meaningful translations of Christian realities, starting with that for the Catholic Church herself.

His personal piety was in the line of the future renewal: "To tell you my personal *taste* . . . I have never been attracted to the many forms of prayer that are so widespread. I am passionately fond of the Gospel, the *Imitation* and, as a prayer, the Missal and Breviary. . . ." But he did not condemn or pour scorn on those with a different "taste", and he claimed (in a letter in 1917) that he was much taken by the rosary when prayed suitably. A little afterward he discovered St. Thèrése of Lisieux and, after founding his Little Sisters, he encouraged them in adopting the "little way".

Is Père Lebbe here simply a "man of his time" as he suggests in his letter of May 1, 1900 to his brother? In this letter he was perhaps only being his age—he was not yet 23 years old. "To stay young"—as he always did—could have meant no more than being fashionable—a leader perhaps or even a creator of fashion, but, by this very fact, unstable and fragile. Prophetic acts are ahead of their time; being eschatological, they must depend on permanent springs. Père Lebbe was therefore a man of the fu-

ture, rooted in traditional values, and recognizing their authenticity and universal application.

Non-Christian Religions and Ecumenism

In the matter of ecumenism, he was by no means fashionable
in his day. From the very first he had the greatest respect for the
multitude of the Chinese and was astounded that so virtuous a
people should not be Christian. By 1906 he was extolling the
asceticism of the Buddhist bonzes. Until his death he was re-
proached by opponents—and also others at times—for his bias
in favor of the Chinese. Such reproach came even from non-
Christians, among whom he had some good friends.

While in Europe he was sometimes asked: "If the Chinese are
so civilized and good, Father, what are you doing as a missionary
among them?" He would reply: "You have missed the point; one
is not there to civilize, but to bring them the one vital thing
which is missing—Christ."

In order to strengthen the faith of his converts and to console
them on the death of a non-baptized relative, he did not hesitate to state that they could be saved. Thus we see him offering
Mass (in private) for the mother of one of his students.

Père Lebbe's sensitive and differentiated attitude toward the
Protestants was clearly the precursor of ecumenism. For example, in 1906, at Cho-Chow, he had a Protestant minister to a
meal—friendliness which earned him a severe rebuke from
Msgr. Jarlin. At the end of July 1919 he went to visit an Irish
member of his order at Ninghai for two months; he explained
why to his brother-in-law: "I am learning English . . . because I wish to meet the American pastors in Shaohin who are
'gentlemen and good fellows'." Between June and December
1925 he used to meet the Anglican missionary Priscilla Barclay
in Paris, and he took his leave of her on November 10, 1925,
writing: "It has been a tremendous pleasure for me to know you
just a little. It will form an unbreakable bond between the Sheng-
kong Kiao and the Sheng-kong Huei" (Anglican and Catholic

Churches—the style follows the original). *The Small Woman* [4] tells in a somewhat romantic fashion of his sympathetic meeting with another British missionary during the war against Japan.

It is symbolic that by Père Lebbe's bedside as he lay dying were to be found, among others, a Protestant journalist and a non-Christian general. And it was this latter who, upon orders from the head of state, gave him the highest mark of honor possible for a Chinese—offering him the most beautiful coffin to be found in Chungking.

Character of Père Lebbe

We have not been able to touch upon many facets of our subject even in passing—for example the originality of his two religious foundations, the encouragement he gave to secular priests to serve in the churches of Africa and Asia, his part in non-Catholic "works", his vital role in the establishment of the Benedictines in China, etc.

Let us underline in conclusion that he was no explosive Savonarola. His letters home show an extreme, almost childlike sensitivity. His frequent demands on his Brothers and Sisters were tempered by the perception of a father. He could joke, full of the joy of life, even in the worst periods of a terrible war.

Final Remark

Is his life really an encouragement? The present situation of the Church in China, it would seem, is very far indeed from the glorious future Père Lebbe had predicted when he said China would have its own independent bishops. Was he then a false prophet?

True, Père Lebbe was an incorrigible optimist. Looking closer, however, one can detect a Jeremiah listened to too late. The consecration of bishops, suggested in 1908, asked for in 1914 and judged urgent in order to avoid a catastrophe in 1917, began at last in 1926; in 1949 the Chinese comprised only one

[4] Alan Burgess, *The Small Woman* (filmed as *The Inn of the Sixth Happiness*).

quarter of the bishops in China! In 1920 he thought wide-ranging action among Chinese students essential, abroad and at home. But what was done was too limited, and from 1928 even this was reduced, Père Lebbe playing practically no part because of his superior's opposition. Unions, recommended since 1912, never got established. As for the rest, one could quote several passages from his letters between 1925-1927, as well as his ideas at the end of his life, which would reveal his consciousness of the seriousness of the approaching situation.

Nevertheless his ideals and his prophetic action are to be seen reflected to no small extent in what Vatican Council II has done and in what must follow from it. Here then, in lieu of conclusion, is a "testimony of an old comrade from the same school", Msgr. Morel, former archbishop of Suiyuan: "It gives me great pleasure to pay honor to the memory of this childhood friend of mine whom God had predestined for an unrewarding mission, to the honor of his Church."

Part II
Documentation
Concilium

Office of the Executive Secretary
Nijmegen, Netherlands

Concilium General Secretariat/*Nijmegen, Netherlands*

Prophets in the Secular City

An earlier volume of *Concilium* [1] has already given a bibliographical survey about the prophets. There Vawter drew attention to the new insights into what is usually meant in Christian language by prophets—men of the Old and the New Testament who, by word and by deed, direct the attention and energies of the believing community toward the future; they were prophets in the City of God. This aspect will not be overlooked in this documentation, although it will concentrate more on prophecy as a general religious phenomenon [2] and on the assertion that the Churches need a new prophecy in order to emerge from the present impasse. [3] The pastoral use of such a documentation seems to be inevitably determined by such practical issues as: (1) Where do we find prophets in what, since

[1] B. Vawter, "Recent Literature on the Prophets," in *Concilium* 10 (1965), pp. 61-67).

[2] R. C. Zaehner, *Inde, Israël, Islam. Religions mystiques et révélations prophétiques* (Paris/Bruges, 1965); T. Spasky, "Le culte du prophète Elie et sa figure dans la tradition orientale," in *Elie le prophète* I (Paris/Bruges, 1956), pp. 219-32; K. Schlosser, *Propheten in Afrika* (Braunschweig, 1949); J. Garcia Trapiello, "Profetismo profesional en el antiguo Israel y en los pueblos vecinos," in *Cultura Biblica* 24 (Madrid, 1967), pp. 138-51; G. Fohrer, "Prophetie und Geschichte," in *Theol. Literaturzeitung* 89/7 (1964), pp. 481-500.

[3] "Le réveil du prophétisme," in *Inf. cath. intern.* 303 (Jan. 1, 1968), pp. 3-12; Cardinal F. König, "Propheten müssen lästig werden," in *Worte zur Zeit* (Vienna, 1968), pp. 249-55.

Harvey Cox, has been called the "secular city" and no longer the "City of God"? (2) What can we do with such prophecy?

Prophecy as a Universal Religious Phenomenon

The history of religion has brought us a better understanding of non-Christian religions and prophecy appears to be a universal religious phenomenon, not solely the privilege of Judaism and Christianity. In his classic work on prophecy,[4] Néher devoted a first section to nonbiblical prophecy. In the old cultures of Egypt, Mesopotamia, Phoenicia, Iran and Greece, prophecy appears to have been considered as important as in Israel. No doubt, one may say that only in Israel does this prophecy lead to the covenant, but this does not explain away the fact that it also operated among the peoples that surrounded Israel. There, too, prophecy plays an essential part in the whole of society. Sometimes, as in Mesopotamia and Phoenicia, the prophet even determined the political course of the country, and prophecy was at the service of the established power.

Nor is it strange that prophecy appears in one form or another in all great religions. For prophecy has to do with the dynamic element of every religion. Genuine religion never stands outside the culture or politics of society but is closely intertwined with it. Religion, too, is expected to contribute to the solution of the problems that confront society—its function, its power, its meaning and its future. Insofar as religion dares to tackle these challenges, it proves its vitality and has a future. When it lets these problems pass by without being involved in them, religion has already outlived its relevancy. The question put by society to religion with regard to the future is then a test case: Does religion offer a vision for the future, or is it merely the protagonist of the *status quo?*

Taken by and large, the history of religion, including that of

---

[4] A. Néher, *L'Essence du prophétisme* (Paris, 1955), pp. 17-81; M. Buber, "Der Glaube der Propheten," in *Werke* II (Munich, 1964), pp. 431 and 459; P. Auvray, "Le prophète comme guetteur," in *Rev. Biblique* 61/2 (1964), pp. 191-205; L. Rost, "Das Problem der Weltmacht in der Prophetie," in *Theol. lit. zeit.* 90 (1965), pp. 241-50.

Christianity, shows three ways in which religion tries to answer this question.

1. Religion pretends to be able to forecast the future. The prophet is then the man who can see the future and tries to predict it. This is probably the most primitive form of prophecy. An obvious disadvantage of this concept of prophecy is that it strips the future in this way of its challenging character which lies precisely in its not being known. Where this kind of prophecy appears, we meet with secondary phenomena which prevent religion from making a positive contribution to the future—namely, incantations and fortune-telling. Such prophecies act rather as a means of comfort and reassurance than as an active urge toward the future.[5]

2. By its dynamic character religion can also reach out toward the future. Then the prophet is the man who refuses to mistake the means for the end. Not satisfied with what has already been achieved, he sees how the material of the past can be used to build up the future. Of this kind of prophecy Moses is the symbol in Israel. Religion then always leads man into the desert and drives him out of the apparent quiet and security of slavery. That is why this kind of prophet is never honored in his own country. He restlessly summons the people to go out and meet the unknown, because there lies the future. This future may be indeterminate but the prophet can pour an evocative power into the symbol of the "promised land" without letting this "promised land" so fully occupy his mind that he forgets the way that must lead to it. This volume of Concilium shows Lebbe and Newman as prophetical figures in this sense. In the same sense Marx is often spoken of as a social prophet.

3. A third way in which religion faces the challenge of the future looks at first sight to be a shifting of the responsibility for this future to someone else—for instance, to God who already knows the whole future and prepares it for those that serve him. In our days this function of God seems to have been taken over

[5] G. Fohrer, "Prophetie und Magie," in *Zeitschr. f. Alttest. Wiss.* 78 (1966), pp. 25-47.

by science. The secular-minded believer will then overrate science and laud it as the true owner of the future; from science these new believers expect the solution of the future just as passively as they formerly expected it of God. In this context the prophet who speaks in the name of God recalls man from every form of idolatry by pointing to man's own responsibility. He is aware of speaking for God, but his first preoccupation is to purge the image man has of God so that it becomes impossible to identify him with a "know-all" who would rob man of his responsibility. He is a man who hopes in the promises of the covenant, never revoked, rather than a man who tries to penetrate into the mystery of God, which is hidden from him, too. In this sense some people call Barth and Bonhoeffer prophets rather than theologians.

Although we have named a few persons as representing these three ways of prophecy, we are well aware of the fact that these ways rarely appear in their pure essence. When, therefore, one speaks today of prophecy in the Church [6] or about the prophetic way as the only way that can enable the Church to remain relevant,[7] the accent does not fall on one of these three separate ways but on the evocative character implied in prophecy.

Yet, even today all these three forms of prophecy still operate in the Church, as the contents of this volume prove. We shall

[6] Y. Congar, *Vraie et fausse réforme dans l'Eglise* (Paris, 1950), pp. 196-226; E. C. Bianchi, "Bonhoeffer and the Church's Prophetic Mission," in *Theological Studies* 28/4 (1967), pp. 801-11: "He felt that the Church was largely unconverted to the prophetism of Scripture. . . . The cleavage between a non-prophetic Church and a world come of age was intensified for Bonhoeffer by Christianity's retreat into religiousness"; A. de Bovis, "Le peuple de Dieu et sa mission prophétique," in *La Vie Spirituelle* 542 (1967), pp. 275-88; P. Ricoeur makes an important distinction between prophecy and eschatology in "Approche philosophique du concept de liberté religieuse," in *L'Herméneutique de la liberté religieuse* (Paris, 1968), p. 217; in this connection we must also mention the beautiful little volume by T. L. Westow, *Introducing Contemporary Catholicism* (London, 1967), pp. 104f.

[7] J. M. González-Ruiz, "Sécularisation et communauté ecclésiale," in *Ido-c* 68-13, 7: "The only possibility for the Church to survive in the secularized world in which we live is the prophetic form."

therefore give first of all some concrete facts which illustrate the presence of these three forms in our own age.

Under the first form of prophecy we would range the apparitions of Lourdes, Fatima, Banneux, etc.[8] Without dealing with the psychological reliability and historical exactness of what is said to have taken place there,[9] we are only interested in the prophetic structure of these apparitions. In the apparitions of Fatima, for instance, the following structure seems to be clear: the menace of the future is felt; communism and material values as well as the constant threat of war and the decline in religious practice are sensed as dangers. The threat, however, is allayed by the vision; the solution comes from elsewhere; on the basis of what one of the little seers appears to have heard or seen, it is accepted that Russia will be converted. It is true that moral effort is not totally absent, since there is a call to prayer, penance and conversion. A closer look, however, shows that the promises corresponding to this moral effort are but the popular padding of an indeterminate hope. Foresight and prediction play an important part, but it is a return to what is known of old; the guarantee for the veracity of the predictions is sought in the miraculous; the verification of the predicted events remains difficult because the historical reliability of the report of what exactly has been predicted has not been checked in a professional manner, and all is left in a haze of devotion and popular belief. Yet, such events retain a prophetic meaning,[10] and in this way, however, primitively and perhaps not reflectively, the challenge of the future to the Church is also understood by the ordinary faithful whose

[8] K. Rahner, *Visionen und Prophezeihungen* (Freiburg i. Br., ³1960); Fr. Bruno, "Puissance de l'Archetype," in *Elie le Prophète* II (Paris/ Bruges, 1956), pp. 11-31.

[9] R. Laurentin, *Bernadette raconte les apparitions* (Paris, 1957-66); idem, *Lourdes. Histoire authentique des apparitions* (Paris, 1961-64).

[10] R. Laurentin, *Sens de Lourdes* (Paris, 1954); idem, Part 6 of *Histoire authentique:* "Les trois dernières apparitions. Sens de l'événement" (Paris, 1964); G. Guariglia, *Prophetismus und Heilserwartungsbewegungen als völkerkundliches und religionsgeschichtliches Problem* (Horn/ Vienna, 1959).

hope is fed by something concrete. It is also understandable that such events do not exactly stimulate the interest of theologians. For one of the tasks of theology is to be the link between the man of the past, of tradition, and the man of the future, the prophet. But what this kind of prophecy offers the theologian is not so much a view of the future as a nostalgic view of the past, dressed up in a vision. Here the future is expected as a repetition of an idealized past.

In the present understanding of the Church the greatest need seems to be for the second kind of prophecy. Pius XII spoke on occasion of the tired Church. This tiredness arises from a feeling of impotence and superfluity in the faithful. They have the impression that the new world is built up without them. They need to be roused from this situation. Here there is room for such prophetic figures as John XXIII, Söderblom, Maximos IV, Helder Camara and others. They not only preach salvation or the lack of it but make it clear at the same time that the faithful have to make a contribution to this Church of tomorrow. They are not so absorbed by the futuristic Church of the year 2000 that it prevents them from taking the right decisions and setting a new course now. They show, however, that this contribution can never be spelt out in detail (cf. Schema XIII). The future cannot be identified with the present moment when we have in fact worked out the plans which the study of the future offers us now.

Planning is certainly indispensable for a future which cannot be waited for in sheer passivity. The mystery of the future, however, is more than the realization of plans made today. We cannot master the future completely; it approaches us also in its own way.[11] The prophet may nevertheless have a vision against a background of what is scientifically foreseeable. Peace, development, macro-ethics and a diaspora Church are more than what can be foreseen by polemology, sociology, economics and human

[11] K. Rahner, "Fragment aus einer theologischen Besinnung auf den Begriff der Zukunft," in *Schriften zur Theologie* VIII (Einsiedeln, 1967), p. 555; J. Pieper, *Hoffnung und Geschichte* (Munich, 1967); P. Schütz, *Parusia—Hoffnung und Prophetie* (Heidelberg, 1960).

maneuvering. The future has a margin of vagueness which cannot be clarified solely by planning but on which such prophetic personalities can cast the light of hope. What is most important then is not what they think or write (this is clear in the writings of John XXIII) but what they do. Here the theologian's function as the link between tradition and prophecy becomes more obvious and is therefore seized upon with greater alacrity.[12] It is curious that in the more recent exegetical studies of the prophetic books of Scripture the person of the prophet stands out more clearly than the text.[13] They aim at finding the person behind the texts. In this context the theologian points not merely to the scientific message for the future (although he will, of course, not neglect it in any sense) but rather to the Christian behind the message, to prevent, as Schillebeeckx puts it, this hope of the future from becoming an escape into the future.[14]

The third kind of prophecy may be said to find a representative today in Teilhard de Chardin. Like every human being the prophet, too, has to struggle with the reality of his age. Does time condition man to such a degree that he is essentially bound to it? Is the phenomenon of man essentially a phenomenon of time? Or is the excessive seriousness with which time is treated in an existential and history-making Christianity one of the factors that may lead to a "forgetfulness of being" (*Seinsvergessenheit*). The popular image of the prophet seems to imply that he can, as it were, ignore time and see behind it. One might possibly say that the prophet makes man aware of the fact that he is not so totally locked up in time that it completely dominates him. Man is not wholly determined by either the present or the past. These are

[12] E. Schillebeeckx, "The Magisterium and the World of Politics," in *Concilium* 36 (1968).

[13] H. Renckens, *De profeet van de nabijheid Gods* (Tielt, 1966); L. Stachel, "Interpretation prophetischer Sprachgestalt auf dem zeitgeschichtlichen Hintergrund," in *Katech. Blätter* 92/10 (1967), pp. 608-15; S. H. Stenson, "Prophecy, Theology and Philosophy," in *Journ. Rel.* 44/1 (1964), pp. 17-28; C. Tresmontant, *La doctrine morale des prophètes d'Israel* (Paris, 1958); R. Kilian, "Die prophetischen Berufungsberichte," in *Theologie im Wandel* (Munich/Freiburg, 197), p. 356.

[14] E. Schillebeeckx, "Het nieuwe Godsbeeld, secularisatie en politiek," in *Tijdschrift voor Theologie* 8/1 (1968), p. 49.

points on which the prophets of the Old Testament insisted constantly.

But man is not wholly determined by the future either. Prophets of today [15] like those of antiquity, those of the City of God and those of the secular city, saw this as the heart of their message. It is a striking fact that the prophets of the scientific revolution warn against a too optimistic view of the future even more gravely than the theologians. Many, therefore, feel that the conquest of time as it emerges in the works of Teilhard [16] implies a too naive optimism, although this is not the case in Teilhard's own vision. Thus exegetes, when dealing with the prophets, will talk about a prophetic perspective that leads beyond time as measurable; theologians will draw attention, with Cullman,[17] to the fact that in the Jewish scriptures the element of time is treated in a way that differs from the way we do it in our civilization, more influenced here by Hellenism; philosophers like Bergson will make a careful distinction between measurable time (*temps*) and "duration" filled with vital human experience (*durée*).[18]

Insofar as believers are concerned, they are not satisfied with an answer that plays about with a notion of eternity as if it were merely endlessly protracted time. This is probably one of the reasons why many find it difficult to accept the preaching of a resurrection, a heaven—in short, man's blessed "duration". Does this not show something of that forgetfulness of being (*Seinsvergessenheit*) [19] which prevents the believer of today from

[15] N. Lohfink, *Profeti ieri e oggi* (Brescia, 1967), p. 134.
[16] B. Charbonneau, *Teilhard de Chardin, prophète d'un âge totalitaire* (Denoël, 1963).
[17] O. Cullmann, *Christus und die Zeit* (Zürich, 1946); idem, *Heil als Geschichte. Heilsgeschichtliche Existenz im Neuen Testament* (Tübingen, 1965).
[18] H. Bergson, *Les deux sources de la morale et de la religion* (Paris, 1932), where the need for prophecy is pointed out for the vitality of any morality and any religion.
[19] "In physics as an exact science the 'understanding of being' (*Seinsverständnis*), of what is now, is reduced to a concept which, because of the structure and bearing of the science, is incapable of seeing the being of, e.g., place, time, movement, force, mass, as a problem in its own right": M. Heidegger, *Das Wesen des Grundes* (Pfullingen, [3]1949), p. 13.

being persuaded of the lastingness of what man is but makes him want to limit salvation to whatever salvation or happiness can be achieved within time?

These three kinds of prophecy show with increasing clarity that the true prophet never deprives man of his responsibility. Buber [20] has pointed out that between prophecy and apocalypse in the Old Testament there is the same difference as between indeterminism and determinism, or between hope and despair. The prophet recoils from the message he is charged with by God, but he yields to the urgency of the message; he grasps it firmly in his hands and in thus committing himself he finds the persuasive strength of his certainty. The apocalyptic seer (Buber refers to the one in Ezra and the author of the Apocalypse) sees himself confronted with a catastrophe from which he perceives no escape. He sees the "new" descend from heaven as an outsider. For him the "new" is already there, but it has not yet found its proper place; for him it descends ready-made from heaven. For the prophet the future is not fixed, but he believes in it and devotes his energies to it. The prophet is constantly in an attitude of dialogue and this leads to a covenant; the apocalyptic seer is always engaged in a monologue even though he presents this monologue as the Word of God. He is not helpful for the vitality of religion.

Buber points out that these two forms never appear in their essential purity and that even the most authentic prophet of Israel, Jeremiah, shows apocalyptic features, while there are prophetic elements in the Apocalypse. The prophet believes in the constant rejuvenation of religion and of the future; the apocalyptic seer has no real future; for him the one situation vanishes, old and worn out, and the next situation simply takes its place.[21]

One could trace the same features in the prophets that have been discussed in this volume. It would also be interesting to

[20] M. Buber, "Prophetie und Apokalyptik," in *Werke* II (Munich, 1964), pp. 930-36.
[21] *Idem*, "Das Problem des Menschen," in *Werke* I, p. 329, where Karl Marx is described as "apocalyptic".

examine how strong the apocalyptic element is in such sects as the Mormons [22] who started under J. Smith as a prophetical movement. They want to restore the Church of Christ but have become isolated from Christianity and have ended up as the tightly organized embodiment of an idealized image of the People of God and the primitive Church. Church history is full of these splinter movements whose fanaticism quenches prophetic power and whose idealization of the past blocks the way to the future. They are not really creative although their activity is admired by all. One has but to think of what has been achieved by the Quakers, the Jehovah's Witnesses, the Moravian Brethren, the Adventists and others.[23] They live, however, on the margin of society and their structure prevents them from being a leaven. They cling to tradition and can only see the future as a menace. One cannot help remembering Jean Guitton's idea that tradition is the future of yesterday and the future is the tradition of tomorrow.[24] In this sense the prophet works on the tradition of tomorrow.

Prophecy is therefore not merely a phenomenon of the past, subject matter for an historian; it is also present momentarily in Christianity. It is significant that the Israelites began to doubt salvation history [25] when there were no more prophets, for then

[22] N. R. Burr, *A Critical Bibliography of Religion in America* I (Princeton, 1961), pp. 324-34; H. Nibley, *The World and the Prophets* (Utah, 1965); C. H. Lalive d'Epinay, "The Pentecostal 'Conquista' in Chile," in *The Ecum. Rev.* 1 (1968), pp. 16-32; W. J. Hollenweger, "Evangelism and Brazilian Pentecostals," in *The Ecum. Rev.* 2 (1968), pp. 163-70.

[23] R. A. Knox, *Enthusiasm* (Oxford, 1950); E. W. Bentz, *Der Prophet Jakob Boehme* (Marburg, 1959).

[24] Quoted in H. Fesquet, *Le catholicisme religion de demain?* (Paris, 1962), p. 214; cf. the penetrating article by G. Casalis, "Réflexions sur le ministère prophétique de l'Eglise," in *Etudes Théol. et Rel.* 41/4 (1966), pp. 227-40; M. de la Croix, "Un prophétisme dans l'Eglise," in *Elie le prophète* II (Paris/Bruges, 1956), pp. 151-89.

[25] S. Hermann, *Die prophetischen Heilserwartungen im Alten Testament. Ursprung und Gestaltwandlung* (Stuttgart, 1965); A. Gonzáles Nuñez, *Profetas, Sacerdotes y Reyes en el antiguo Israel* (Madrid, 1963); R. Lazzarini, "Ermeneutica profetica della tradizione," in *Arch. Filos. Ital.* 1-2 (1963), pp. 323-42; J. Lindblom, *Prophecy in Ancient Israel* (Oxford, 1962).

there is no more future. True salvation is no longer present when one feels threatened by annihilation. The abandoning of the Church which we experience at the moment, particularly the abandonment of ecclesiastical office, might well be due for a large part to the scarcity of prophets.[26] It is precisely the purpose of a documentation like this article to show that there is genuine prophecy in the Church, prophets who are difficult and make life difficult for others, but who, because of their hope in the future, remain within the Church. The awkwardness of the prophets sometimes makes it a problem how to use them, a problem which we must mention in more detail.

The Usefulness of Prophets in the Secular City

We have pointed to the presence of prophets in the Church, but not in order to tempt the reader to let himself slide back into a comforting feeling that now everything will be all right with the Church. Occasionally the word of the prophets is not heard. A striking case is the work by Rosmini on the five wounds of the Church.[27] This voice was heard only more than a century later and is unfortunately still as relevant as it was then. There are nevertheless certain forms of prophecy which can no longer serve the Christian awakening to the future. Following Néher [28] we suggest, therefore, a few distinctions in prophecy.

First of all, there is a magic prophecy. This tries to cover up the threat of the future with mere words. It is usually at the

[26] J. Grandmaison, Crise de prophétisme. Spiritualité du laicat (Montreal, 1965); T. Michels, "Propheten und prophetische Bekenntnis in der Kirche," in Wahrheit und Verkündigung (Munich, 1967); L. Festinger, H. W. Riecken and S. Schlachter, When Prophecy Fails (Minneapolis, 1956); J. W. Schulte Noordholt, "De leider," in Wending 22/1 (1967), pp. 604-05.
[27] A. Rosmini, Delle cinque piaghe della Santa Chiesa (Lugano, 1848); C. Leetham, "Die fünf Wunden der Kirche," in Orientierung 32/6 (1968), pp. 72-75. The "five wounds" are: the gap between people and clergy through language and liturgy; inadequate theological training of the priests; lack of collegiality among bishops; the intertwining of State and Church, politics and pastoral care; the Church's clinging to property. The ecclesiastical condemnation of this book was quashed last year; a new edition appeared which was sold out within two months.
[28] See note 4.

service of the dominant class or a given dynasty.[29] The prophecy of the indestructibility of the Church has often been manipulated in this way, to the disadvantage of the Church. The religious movement behind Black Power is also clearly a prophecy at the service of a definite power, and this distinguishes it unfavorably from another prophetic movement in the same field, that of the late Martin Luther King.[30]

Second, there is, according to Néher, social prophecy. It works usually in support of an ideal ethics or politics. Altizer [31] has pointed out that the concept of "God's own country" to describe the U.S.A. has had great influence (both good and bad) on the formation of America's social conscience. In the same way the Old Testament prophecy of the promised land has been used today politically at the origin of the State of Israel.[32] Social prophecy always plays on people's ideal or idealized needs, and always operates in favor of something different. These prophecies all have something chiliastic about them, some vague longing for some millennium. Perhaps the magic number of the year 2000 has something to do with it.

Critical reflection makes one ask whence the prophet draws his vision, his word, his hope of the future. The answer usually points to an intuitive knowledge, a being "tuned in" on God's designs, a sympathy. And in this sense people talk about a mystical prophecy.[33] There is always a moment of experience in

---

[29] H. J. Kraus, *Prophetie und Politik* (Munich, 1952); G. Zizola, "Politique et prophétisme," in *Inf. cath. intern.* 305 (1968), pp. 8-10; C. Loubet, *Savonarole, prophète assassiné* (Paris, 1967); W. von Soden, "Verkündigung des Gotteswillens durch prophetisches Wort in den Altbabylonischen Briefen aus Mari," in *Die Welt des Orients* 1 (1950), pp. 397-403.

[30] Martin Luther King, *Chaos or Community?* (New York, 1967).

[31] T. J. J. Altizer, "Amerikas Schicksal und der Tod Gottes," in *Antaios* 9/5 (1968), pp. 483-99.

[32] G. Fohrer, "Israels Haltung gegenüber den Kanaänäern," in *Journal of Semitic Studies* 13/1 (1968), pp. 70-71.

[33] H. Knight, *The Hebrew Prophetic Consciousness* (London, 1957); J. Lindblom, *op. cit.*, overcomes the distinction between prophets belonging to a cult and free prophets by concentrating on religious experience; H. H. Rowley, "The Nature of O.T. Prophecy in the Light of Recent Study," in *The Servant of the Lord* (1952), p. 91; H. Widengrin, *Literary*

Christianity. It may be discredited today, but the history of the Church constantly shows up figures such as Ruusbroec, Ignatius of Loyola, Teresa of Avila, Berdyaev, Charles de Foucauld and Patriarch Maximos [34] who drew from their religious experience a message for the Church which opened up a new future. There is, however, a not wholly imaginary danger that less genuine religious experiences than those of the true mystics, such as those of seers and others, may be exploited consciously or subconsciously by the ecclesiastical or secular establishments.

David Flusser [35] maintains that Christianity has emasculated the messianic prophecy through its dogmatized belief that the messianic expectations have been realized in Jesus. This contains a grain of truth insofar as Christians are inclined to read the New Testament as detached from the Old and therefore do not see Christ sufficiently in the perspective of the prophets of the Old Testament. One cannot sufficiently take to heart what Barth wrote in the fourth volume of his *Dogmatik* (3, 1): "In earlier and later ages it has often been suggested and attempted either to shake off the so-called Old Testament altogether or at least to reduce it to the level of a good and useful deutero-canonical introduction to the real Bible, namely the New Testament. Over against this one cannot realize clearly enough that for the earliest Church, among the Gentiles as well as among the Jews, it was not the Old Testament that was the 'added complement' but the New; it was the New Testament that was the addition to and extension of the canon; this canon was that of the synagogue: Moses, the prophets and the psalms (Lk. 24, 44) and was the

---

and Psychological Aspects of the Hebrew Prophets (Uppsala/Leipzig, 1948); W. M. W. Roth, "The Anonymity of the Suffering Servant," in Journ. of Bibl. Lit. 83/2 (1964), pp. 171-79, establishes a direct relationship between God and the prophet.

[34] M. Villain, "Un prophète: Maximos IV," in *Nouv. Rev. Théol.* 90/1 (1968), pp. 50-66.

[35] D. Flusser, *De joodse oorsprong van het christendom* (Amsterdam, 1964), p. 15; H. J. Schoeps, *Israel und die Christenheit* (Frankfurt, ²1961); K. H. Rengstdorf and S. von Korzfleisch, *Kirche und Synagoge. Handbuch zur Geschichte von Christen und Juden* I (Stuttgart, 1968), pp. 30-34 and 307-58.

undoubted nucleus of their Holy Scripture." [36] The practice today is that, however deeply the Church believes that in Jesus, God's last prophetic Word to man has been spoken, this Word still constantly needs new men to bring deeper understanding and new prophets who summon us by their inspiration to new progress. We still expect the "pleroma" of Christ, the fulfillment. As to whether Teilhard's vision of Christ was theologically exact as the Omega point, one had better ask those conversant with modern christology, but his vision has prophetically stimulated many Christians to look over the wall of faith at what is taking place in the scientific field and even to demolish here and there walls of separation built up during the course of centuries.

One of the least appreciated results has been the prophetic voice with which scientists and the sciences begin to speak to the Churches and the theologians. C. J. Dippel [37] and others deserve credit for having drawn our attention to this. A number of scientists see more and more clearly that the slogan of a "neutral" science, not concerned with values, has become a myth that is out of date. They are faced with a responsibility which they cannot bear on the basis of science alone. Outsiders may still look up to science as the new god, the new omnipotence. But science itself has become more and more conscious of the fact that it is at the service of politics and economics. Physical sciences and technical know-how are in danger of being used by structures that can only widen the gap between poor and rich, developed and underdeveloped, and constantly give the collective egotism of the States new opportunities for aggression or war. Technical achievement and the direction of scientific research must be controlled by some authority beyond the sciences.

The direction of scientific development is not the result of an option made by scientists but is dictated in a barely concealed

---

[36] J. Coppens, "Le Messianisme Royal," in *Nouv. Rev. Théol.* 190/5 (1968), pp. 479-512, gives an abundant bibliography on messianic prophecy.

[37] C. J. Dippel, *Wijsgerige en ethische aspecten der Natuurwetenschap.* This is Vol. II of *Geloof en Natuurwetenschap* by the Study Commission of the Dutch Reformed Church (The Hague, 1968).

way by politics and economics. Some of these scientists have realized that the ideal of "pure science" is an illusion and that they are being manipulated by powers outside the scientific field so that science itself is deprived of responsibility. Moreover, none of these power structures can fit this scientific development into a universalist perspective. And this makes some of these scientists wonder whether this perspective cannot be found in the message of salvation. Thus Dippel shows that, while within the Church there is hardly any understanding for this kind of problem, the scientists are confronted every day with a whole mass of concrete evangelical decisions in which they have to make clear, in very secular and non-religious terms, what they mean; they have to choose in order to see to it that life remains human and the secularizing world does not destroy itself.

According to Saris [38] a number of prominent scientists have been calling on mankind to be converted, for the end of the world is near. [39] Most of them are not Christians. One recognizes every kind of Old Testament prophecy in their conduct and in the reaction to their conduct. They are not listened to by the majority of people and the authorities, whether believing or not. They are ridiculed and mocked as people who make a lot of unnecessary fuss. One does not know what they are talking about. And so people prefer indifference and irresponsibility and pursue their daily cares and pleasures.

When the Church sees herself, in *Lumen gentium,* as a prophetic people sharing in the prophetic function of Christ,[40] one can only acclaim this prophetic note, however shy it may sound. In this context one may wonder whether it is not the task

[38] B. F. Saris, "Modern profetisme," in *De Bazuin* 51/24 (1968), pp. 6-7. We are grateful to A. Weiler, B. F. Saris and C. J. Dippel for taking part in a colloquy on this new prophecy organized by the General Secretariat.

[39] In this connection we refer to the publications of the Pugwash Conferences in which scientists from all over the world take part. They began in 1955 with the declaration by Russell and Einstein on the explosion of the H bomb.

[40] M. D. Chenu, "Un peuple prophétique," in *Esprit* 35/362 (1967), pp. 602-11.

of theology to elicit, precisely among scientists, these issues of scientific responsibility and not allow them to remain buried under a mythical overestimation with which scientists themselves are far from happy. These issues will begin to operate also within the Churches as a prophetic necessity. No doubt, the Churches cannot pretend to have ready-made answers to these issues or sell their doctrinal system as a convenient home to the scientists, but the message of the Gospel can bring some clarity about human responsibility into the new situation. Some [41] see the *rapprochement* between particularly American theology and analytical philosophy in this light. Existentialism has failed to inspire those involved in the exact sciences who demand a philosophical background to the exercise of their scientific functions. The result has been that out of the exact sciences, mathematics and the physical sciences, a philosophy has sprung up based on language and logic. This analytical philosophy now moves into fields where neo-positivism with its limited principle of verification could not lead to meaningful statements, as in ethics, metaphysics and also theology. This might make theological thought not only more progressive but also more modern and bring about a better mutual understanding between what may be called the humanities and the exact sciences.

In any case the exact sciences are undergoing a crisis which postulates elements other than those contained within these sciences. Picht,[42] who like C. F. von Weizäcker has explained these new problems in the German language, has made an explicit appeal here to the Churches as the exponents of the Gospel. He shows how the sciences have—rightly—disentangled themselves from theological tutelage and then from the whole field of philosophy, thus achieving their autonomy. He wonders, however, whether this has not led to a type of man who has become

[41] M. Jeuken, "Een manco van onze theologie," in *Streven* 8 (1968), pp. 780-83.
[42] G. Picht, *Der Gott der Philosophen und die Wissenschaft der Neuzeit* (Stuttgart, 1966): "Struktur und Verantwortung der Wissenschaft im 20. Jahrhundert," pp. 68-106.

both knowledgeable and powerful as a result of enlightenment and the sciences, but has no longer the freedom to use this knowledge and this power for a universal purpose. Such people will no longer conceal the fact that, while the results of science made it possible to set up structures in politics and economics, they can no longer control whether this will lead to salvation or disaster. They find in themselves no principle by which they can understand the world as a whole from the point of view of its future.[43] Hence they appeal to the universalism of the Gospel.

This should of course not be understood as if the scientists are on a pilgrimage to Canossa, as if they want to put themselves again under the tutelage of theology. Such people as Dippel and Picht are convinced that theological awareness has fallen behind the universality of the Gospel. The expertise, offered by the sciences, can help theology to get closer to the universality of the Gospel.[44] Such authors are well aware of the fact that this situation may lead into two directions, an option for total nihilism or a new possibility for the future, as referred to above.

Only a relatively small group of Christians has so far understood this. Yet, it seems a genuine prophetic utterance which cannot be ignored. In the days that prophets were scarce in Israel it was said that Samuel let no crumb of God's Word fall to the ground. This holds good today. Both inside and outside the Church prophets of disaster are predicting the speedy disintegration of the Church. As causes they point to demythologization, desacralization, loss of authority, lack of discipline among the clergy, the influence of strange theologies and rationalistic sciences, the end of the missionary spirit, the futile dialogue with people who have another philosophy of life, the decline of the essential faith through humanism and the lighthearted rejection of political protection and support. These prophets of doom talk about a deadly crisis and, without noticing it, provoke it: they stimulate the evil. The voice of the sciences, however, produces a

[43] *Idem, Die Verantwortung des Geistes* (Olten/Freiburg, 1965).
[44] G. Howe, *Technik und Strategie im Atomzeitalter* (Witten/Berlin, 1965).

more positive sound, and the meaning of faith at the moment is for modern man that there is a way out of this distress.

In this documentation we have talked of the presence of prophets, even in this age of ours, inside and outside the Church, their usefulness and the need for them in the critical situation of the Churches. We cannot conclude this documentation more fittingly than by quoting the unconscious characterization of the prophet by one of the rare prophets of today, Martin Luther King, who had to pay the price paid by so many prophets: "I prefer to be a man with a conviction rather than a man who follows the majority. Now and then one develops a conviction in one's life which is so valuable and full of meaning that one clings to it to the end. If all negroes in the United States were converted to violence, I would prefer to remain the sole and solitary voice to preach that this is the wrong way."

Such words and gestures must be understood and seen without suspicion within the official Church. The suspicion of prophecy has led to the formation of the so-called sects, especially outside the official Church. What could only develop and become manifest with great difficulty within the Church developed on the periphery of Christendom and showed itself mainly outside the Church's official boundaries. This is why the so-called sects are called the unpaid bills and the stepchildren of Christianity. It is, however, a sign of hope that in recent years some of their leading figures have joined in with the ecumenical movement.[45]

[45] G. Barauna and others, *De Kerk van Vaticanum II*, Vol. I (Bilthoven, 1966); P. A. van Leeuwen, "De algemene deelname aan het profetisch ambt van Christus," *ibid.*, pp. 479-506.

BIOGRAPHICAL NOTES

ROGER AUBERT was born on January 16, 1914 in Belgium and ordained in 1938. He studied at the University of Louvain, where he obtained doctorates in history of philosophy (1933) theology (1942) and his M.A. in theology (1945). He is also a doctor *honoris causa* of the University of Nijmegen and of the University of the Sacred Heart in Milan. He has been professor of church history at Louvain since 1952, and is editor of *Revue d'Histoire Ecclésiastique* and *Dictionnaire d'Histoire et de Geographie Ecclésiastiques*. Among his important publications are a new and enlarged edition of *Le Pontificat de Pie IX*, Vol. XXI of *l'Histoire de l'Eglise des origines jusqu'à nos jours*, (Paris 1964) and *Vatican I*, Vol. XII of *l'Histoire des Conciles Oecumeniques*, (Paris 1964).

GIULIO BASETTI-SANI, O.F.M. was born on January 6, 1912 in Florence and ordained in 1935. He studied at the Catholic Institute of Paris, the Institute of Oriental Studies in Rome, the Catholic Faculty of Lyon, the Institute of Islamic Studies at McGill University, Canada, and at Dropsie College, Philadelphia, U.S.A. He is a lecturer on Eastern ecclesiastical studies, also in theology and philosophy, and has a degree for Copt and Arabic. He is guest-professor at the University of Saint Bonaventure in New York and at the University of Notre Dame, Indiana, U.S.A. His published works include *Mohammed and St. Francis* (Ottawa 1959), and *Introduzione allo Studio del Corano* (Brescia 1967). He is a noted contributor to *Revue d'Histoire Ecclésiastique* (Louvain) and to *Studi Francescani* (Florence).

ELISABETH BEHR-SIGEL was born in France on July 21, 1907, and is a member of the Orthodox Church. She studied at the University of Strasbourg and at the theology faculty in Paris, obtaining degrees in philosophy and theology and a teaching certificate for philosophy. She lectures in philosophy and psychopedagogy at the Ecole Normale de Nancy Maxéville in France. Her published works include *Prière et Sainteté dans l'Eglise Russe* (Paris 1950) and a number of articles on spirituality in the Orthodox Church. She is a frequent contributor to *Contacts* and *Messager Orthodoxe*.

CHARLES DESSAIN, CONG. ORAT., was born on September 2, 1907 in England. He studied at Balliol College, Oxford and obtained his M.A. in history. He is one of the most eminent specialists on Newman, and edited *The Letters and Diaries of John Henry Newman*, of which Vols. XI and XVII appeared in London between 1961 and 1967. He is also the author of *John Henry Newman* (London 1967).

WILLIAM PETERS, S.J. was born on April 16, 1911 in Nijmegen, Holland and ordained in 1942. He studied at Heythrop College, England, at

Maestricht, and at the University of Amsterdam. He is a D.Litt. in English, and professor of English and of ascetic and mystical theology. He is one of the most eminent specialists on the *Exercises of Saint Ignatius,* and is the author of *The Spiritual Exercises of St. Ignatius: Exposition and Interpretation* (Jersey City, U.S.A. 1968). He has also written numerous articles on spiritual and religious life in England.

OLIVIER ROUSSEAU, O.S.B. was born in Belgium, February 11, 1898. He was ordained in 1922. He studied at the Anselmo and is editor of *Irénikon* and the author of various books, including *Monarchisme et vie religieuse* (1957) and *L'Orthodoxie et le mouvement oecuménique de 1920 à 1940* (*Ephem. theol. Lovan* 4, 1966).

GORDON RUPP was born on January 4, 1910 in London, and is a Methodist Minister. He studied at London University, at Cambridge, Strasbourg and Basle. He is an M.A. and a doctor of theology, and also doctor of theology (*honoris causa*) at the University of Aberdeen and at the Protestant Faculty of Theology in Paris. He was professor of church history at Manchester University from 1956 to 1967. He is one of the editors of *History of the Methodist Church in Great Britain* (1965).

ALBERT SOHIER, S.A.M. was born on July 19, 1915 at Lubumbasho in the Congo and was ordained in 1938. He studied at the Institute of Philosophy at Louvain, at the Jesuit theological faculty in Louvain, and at the Gregorian in Rome. He obtained his degree in philosophy and doctorate in theology (1944). He has held various posts in lecturing and editing in China and Rouanda. At present he is professor of religion at two institutions in Brussels. He collaborated with P. Goffart in publishing *Lettres de Père Lebbe* (Tournai-Paris 1960), and has contributed to *Bilan du Monde* (Tournai-Paris 1964).

International Publishers of CONCILIUM

ENGLISH EDITION
Paulist Press
Glen Rock, N. J., U.S.A.
Burns & Oates Ltd.
25 Ashley Place
London, S.W.1

DUTCH EDITION
Uitgeverij Paul Brand, N. V.
Hilversum, Netherlands

FRENCH EDITION
Maison Mame
Tours/Paris, France

JAPANESE EDITION (PARTIAL)
Nansôsha
Tokyo, Japan

GERMAN EDITION
Verlagsanstalt Benziger & Co., A.G.
Einsiedeln, Switzerland
Matthias Grunewald-Verlag
Mainz, W. Germany

SPANISH EDITION
Ediciones Guadarrama
Madrid, Spain

PORTUGUESE EDITION
Livraria Morais Editora, Ltda.
Lisbon, Portugal

ITALIAN EDITION
Editrice Queriniana
Brescia, Italy